This book is to be returned on or before
the last date stamped

D0492040

Learn to
PAINT
DR&AW

ACKNOWLEDGEMENTS

The publishers would like to thank the following for permission to reproduce their photographs:

David Astin: 136, 140, 144, 146, 152; Barnaby's Picture Library: 158; Colour Library International: 69, 82, 84, 86, 90; The Trustees of the National Gallery: 9 (below), 54, 55 (below), 56, 81 (below), 95; The Tate Gallery: 57, 58, 73

Illustrations provided by: David Astin: 131–160; Paul Chapelle: 39 (above); Malcolm Henwood: 61 (below) 62, 63 (above), 64 (below), 65 (below), 66, 67 (below), 68, 72, 81 (top), 82 (above), 84 (above), 93 (above), 94; Tudor Humphries: 78, 79, 86, 87, 88, 89; Brian Liddle: 8, 9 (above), 11 (below), 14, 15, 20–9, 32–8, 39 (below), 42–7, 50, 51 (above); Samuel Marshall: 40, 41, 96–105, 108–31; Martin Reiner: 69, 70, 71, 74, 75; Gavin Rowe: 60, 61 (above); Andrew Skilleter: 83; Roger Swanborough: 30 (right), 31, 53; John Thompson: 48, 49, 64 (above), 65 (above), 85; Michael Vicary: 80, 81 (centre); T. W. Ward: 106, 107; Paul Wright: 63 (below), 66 (above, left), 67 (above), 76, 77, 90, 91, 92, 93 (below); Alex Zwarenstein: 7, 10, 11, 12, 13 (above), 16–19, 51 (below).

Graphic artwork by Terry Burton, Liz Chapman, Imperial Artists and Tony Streek.

Text by David Astin (pages 132–60), Alfred Daniels (pages 60–95), Brian Liddle (pages 6–59) and Samuel Marshall (pages 96–131).

The publishers gratefully acknowledge textual contributions to Chapter 1 by Alex Zwarenstein and Roger Swanborough.

Published by Victoria House Publishing Limited, 4/5 Lower Borough Walls, Bath BA1 1QR.

Copyright © 1981 Victoria House Publishing Limited

The material in this book was first published in 1981 as four volumes by Victoria House Publishing Limited.

ISBN 0 907874 06 1

Printed in Hong Kong.

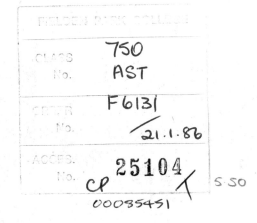

Learn to
PAINT
DRAW &

V H

CONTENTS

Introduction

When given a pencil and a sheet of paper, a child naturally asks the simple question "What shall I draw?" For the aspiring artist, however, the same question becomes far more complicated: "Is it better to start to draw with pencil, charcoal or inks? And is it easier to start painting landscapes with watercolour or oils?" *Learn to Paint and Draw* is written and illustrated by practising artists, and is designed to provide all the information the beginner needs to know, both about materials and techniques.

The important starting-point in drawing and painting is a good working knowledge of the various materials available. The opening chapter not only describes these, but gives step-by-step illustrations to guide you through the actual process of painting various types of subject. Subsequent chapters cover individual themes, each explaining in simple terms the problems of light and shade, the principles of composition and the rules of perspective. By dispelling the mysteries which traditionally surround these elements of drawing and painting, the book will encourage the reader to tackle each subject in a practical and creative way, exploring and developing both skills and imagination.

TECHNIQUES

Why learn techniques?

Every work of art incorporates a degree of technical knowledge and the manipulation of materials to convey a personal message. Technical knowledge may be defined as the ability to carry out the processes which produce the actual work of art. Into this area falls the knowledge necessary to select the materials and prepare the surfaces which will enable the artist to proceed, confident in the knowledge that what he is doing will have the degree of permanence he requires.

In some notable cases the desire to acquire and apply new techniques has led painters to dangerous practices. Perhaps the most famous example was the widespread use, in Victorian oil paintings, of a bituminous black, used to darken the tone in paintings and achieve the appearance of an Old Master. This not only discoloured the oils, but subsequent shrinking during drying caused cracking in many paintings. Most traditional supports are susceptible to temperature and atmospheric variations, and the large departments devoted to the constant repair and renovation of masterpieces in all major galleries testify to the essential impermanence of any painted surface.

Right above and below: Used as washes, ink is capable of conveying a complete and specific tonal range. Used with a pen it gives an incisiveness no other portable medium can approach.
Far right above and below: Watercolour with its ease of use and sensitivity to the paper surface, wide range of colour and glazing capabilities is the ideal medium for sketching but with practice it is capable of major works of art from sketchbook size to large scale.

However, one can ensure by careful method that colours will maintain their density and brightness and that surfaces will not warp and deteriorate at a pace which cannot, with expert care, be reasonably controlled.

Artistic techniques – that is, the methods used to apply the media to the surface – are part and parcel of the artist's uniqueness. Personal techniques should develop out of a search for the means which best serve the individual artist's intentions. However, before arriving at a mature personal statement, which may indeed involve the rejection of orthodox methods, it is usual for the artist to acquire some knowledge of the basic, traditional media and methods. Technical knowledge is evident in any major collection of art, and the student should not only read about and practise his art but also carefully analyze original works of the

great artists. Oil painting technique was perfected by the Dutch, and they have produced many of the leading artists in this field throughout the centuries. Van Eyck, Rembrandt, Vermeer, and Van Gogh should all be studied. Their personal techniques have been major factors in the development of subsequent generations of artists. In the field of watercolor painting, look at the work of the nineteenth-century English masters, Cotman, Turner, Constable, Cox, and the great American masters of the nineteenth and twentieth centuries, Prendergast, Winslow Homer, Bellows, John Singer Sargent and Hopper. With masterly techniques they were able to achieve, in their chosen media, whatever they desired.

Above: *An example of the kind of brisk, direct brushwork, often painting "wet into wet", that would have been used by Van Gogh.*

Right: The Sunflowers, *perhaps the best known of Van Gogh's motifs, shows his painting technique at its peak. Van Gogh spoke of the flowers fading quickly and having to do the "whole thing in one rush". It is unlikely that Van Gogh found it necessary to draw in the whole motif first with charcoal; the drawing and colouring are of the "alla prima" or first time method. Repainting is superfluous.*

Lead pencil

Pencil is one of the most flexible mediums that the artist has at his disposal. It is easily transportable without being messy, can be erased, can be incisive and hard, or soft and sympath-etic, and, in conjunction with a sketch pad or other suitable surface, can always be on hand for drawing and sketching.

The subject matter will often suggest the type of pencil to be used; a soft, misty landscape may dictate the use of a soft pencil, used on its side to make a

Above: *A brisk broken treatment completes the modelling of the figure, again working with two grades.*

Left and below: *Subtle crosshatch using HB and F pencils.*

soft, diffuse mark, while the characterization of an old man's face may suggest a linear rendering with a harder grade of pencil. With this in mind, build up a collection of lead or graphite pencils from the very softest at 8B to the hardest at 9H. At the soft end of the range of graphite pencils, a 6B gives a very soft, fluid line when the point is used and a flat tonal area when the side of the point is used.

The middle range, HB, B, and 2B, are useful for a drawing that you wish to sustain over a long period—a day's landscape drawing or a life class of several hours duration. Start off with a

very light underdrawing, gradually building up the tone with the
B and 2B pencils when you are
confident that the proportions
are correct. A 2H pencil is useful
for light underdrawing. These
pencils should be kept sharp
because their prime characteristic is incisiveness. Also, a
pencil that most draughtsmen
find indispensable is the F
grade, which strikes a balance
between hardness and softness,
and is the ideal sketching pencil.

Carbon and other pencils

Compared to the common lead
or graphite pencil, carbon pencils, available in grades of hard
to soft, give a blacker, chalkier

*The studies on this page show the
different effects and moods which
can be achieved using medium to
soft grades of pencil. Underneath
each main picture is a detail
showing the actual pencil strength.
Moving left to right from the top the
grades used are: F, HB, B, 3B and 5B.*

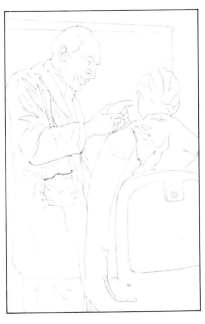

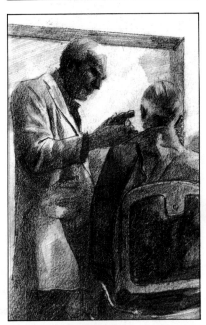

line which can be diffused with an eraser or paper stump. There are also the black conté pencils in three grades: No.1 (medium) No.2 (soft), and No.3 (extra soft), which give a very interesting quality of mark, a little greasier than carbon, not quite as easily diffused, but capable of great depth; a line can be gone over several times, becoming richer and darker in quality. Another plus for the conté pencil and its equivalent conté crayon is that they come in harmonious earth colours — red sanguine, sepia, and bistre, as well as white.

There are many other types of pencil available, including clutch pencils, graphite sticks, and mechanical pencils and holders, which are worth experimenting with for their different qualities of mark and handling.

Above: *Very sharp F and HB pencils were used lightly to convey the essential qualities of a ballerina. Erasing should be avoided in a drawing of this nature, which depends on delicacy of line.*

Above: *Using pencil grades from H to 3B, subtle modulations of tone are achieved in this study by predominant use of continuous shading using the side of the point, rather than crosshatching.*

Charcoal

Charcoal, in the traditional form of willow or vine charcoal sticks, is the oldest drawing medium, and, for the beginner, is most successfully employed for larger drawings. Whereas the pencil mark can be very tightly controlled, a large charcoal drawing demands broader treatment. The special quality of charcoal is its ability to cover large areas quickly and to be erased by simply dusting off the page. It is a wonderful medium for inspiring drawing confidence because of its flexibility and unfussiness, and these qualities should be enjoyed. For detailed drawing, a hard grade charcoal pencil will give the best results.

Paper and tools

A sharpener, heavy-handled cutting knife, or craft knife

Left: *An unsharpened B pencil was used very lightly to give a soft edge effect. Although "unfinished", no further work is required for a satisfactory picture.*

Above: *A complete contrast of mood is seen in this picture, where vigorous use is made of 4B and 6B pencils. A hard surface paper was chosen to maintain the heavy black qualities of the lead.*

Above: *F and B pencils were used in this drawing, which contains many subtle and difficult passages. The pencils were kept very sharp, shading essentially by the continuous tone technique.*

Above: *The motif suggested the use of conté crayons with their range of earth-coloured tones. Conté crayons can be sharpened to a point, but cannot be used over or together with lead pencil.*

should be to hand to keep pencils in optimum working condition. An eraser is also important, not only for erasing mistakes, but also for blending and lifting out lines using the edge or point. There are several types of eraser available; natural, gum, plastic, and kneaded. The natural erasers come in grades of softness, the harder ones being useful for taking out deeply incised lines, the softer for softer lines and charcoal. A kneaded eraser is also useful and can be shaped to suit requirements.

Other erasers should be kept clean by rubbing them on a clean piece of paper, to avoid spoiling the drawing.

The mark the pencil makes will be affected by the grain of the paper and the hardness of its surface. A hard pencil, (any of the H range) will work best on a fine-grained paper. A soft, dark pencil, although quite suitable

Left: *Using a middle grade of black conté pencil a rich tonal effect can be achieved as well as the necessary sharpness in defining the features.*

for a fine-grained paper, is very effective on a rougher grain, giving a textured quality. Scale will, of course, determine the grade of pencil used; a small technical drawing will require a hard pencil and therefore a fine-grained paper.

Coloured papers can extend the range of possible effects. Do not choose a dark tone of paper, unless you intend to use white for the highlights, or the drawing will lose its impact.

Drawing by use of point-relationship

Though some basic understanding of the laws of perspective are helpful to the artist, conveying a three-dimensional scene onto a two-dimensional surface can be achieved quite successfully by drawing using the point-relationship method. The shape and size of the paper or canvas must be able to contain the motif. For example, in

this drawing it was quickly apparent that the motif could be contained in a square and that the boat was tilted slightly to the right. First, draw a vertical line down through the centre of the paper or canvas. This should correspond with the centre of

The four drawings of a boat on these pages demonstrate an easy way of building up a picture accurately without a formal knowledge of perspective.

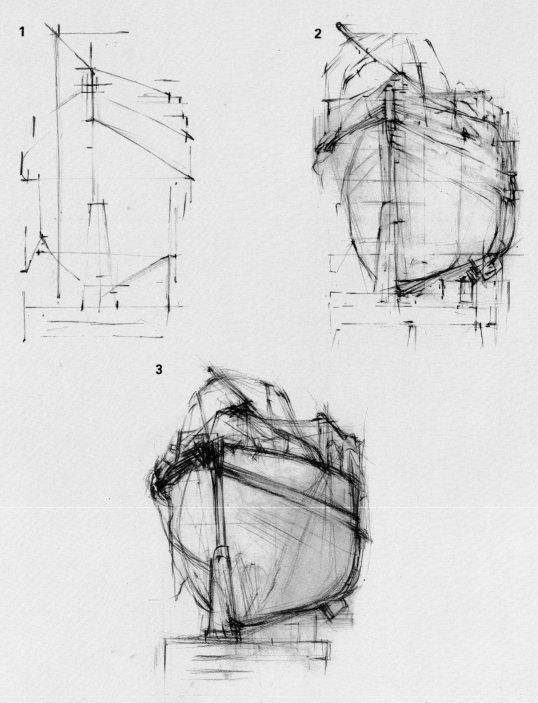

the motif and is also the centre of vision. Holding the pencil at arm's length, use it to measure across the motif to determine how many lengths of the pencil are needed to define the extremities of the subject. Working either side of the centre line, and also along the centre line itself, you will be able to establish the top and bottom limits of the drawing.

When these points have been fixed, use the pencil to deter-mine the angles of the main features. Move across the motif in all directions, measuring distances and relative sizes. A spider's web of marks fixing internal features and sub-divisions will result. Although the objects in front of you may be foreshortened, distances, heights, and recessional depths can be determined and fixed with confidence.

As you include in the drawing the finer details of the subject, the web of lines used to plot the drawing can either be erased or, preferably, absorbed into the drawing. Begin to convey volume by shading in the mass areas.

Should the drawing be the basis for a painting, a brush should be used at this point to block in the main masses and tonal areas. First, however, you should rub down or dust off the pencil or charcoal so that it will not dirty the paint.

4

Coloured pencil

Coloured pencils have come into their own as a serious artistic medium due to the advent of the new, less inhibited styles of the Pop artists. The informality of coloured pencil, previously regarded as a pleasant and straightforward marker for children, is capable of a very wide range of applications in the hands of an expert.

A tremendous range of colours is available. These can be overlaid in a glaze technique and can also be laid flat to give bright, opaque areas. The blending possibilities have been exploited by commercial illustrators to a breathtaking degree of photo-realism, while the humorous, elegant, and decorative drawings of David Hockney illustrate a very different approach.

There are also several brands of water-soluble pencils. As the name implies, these can be turned into a watercolour medium, either by dipping the pencil in water as one works or by first completing the work and then brushing water over it to blend the colours. The pencils are available in packs and are also sold separately so suitable colours can be selected. A full range of greens from one manufacturer may have two or three gaps which can be filled by greens

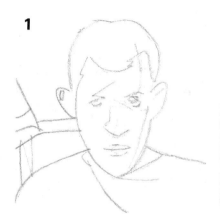

Above: *A wide range of pencil colours is available.*

Left: *In the first drawing, a light blue was used to determine the larger shapes of the figure. In the second, a fine colouring determined the predominant local colour of each area. In the third stage, overlays of warm colours built up the flesh tones while cool colours were used in the shadows.*

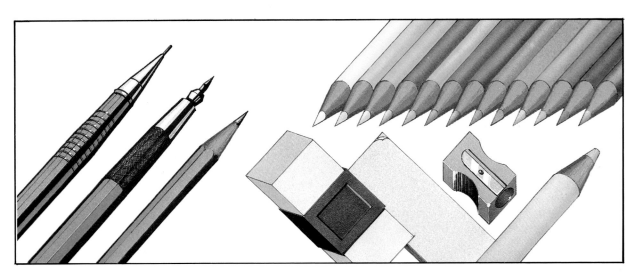

from another manufacturer.

Many types of paper are suitable for coloured pencils but a smooth white drawing paper is perhaps the best. The paper should not be too highly glazed,

Above: *A range of mechanical lead pencils and the most-used coloured pencils, together with various tools for erasing and sharpening.*

Right: *Detail in the face is carefully worked up, preserving it as the focus of interest while the rest is allowed to disintegrate.*

Below: *Do not be afraid to work without preliminary drawing, altering the forms until correct.*

so that the pencil mark will not skid. A hard, white paper will give brilliance, grained papers texture, and coloured papers are best for "mood" drawings. Dark, subdued papers can be very effective, giving an added brilliance to the colours.

To remove mistakes, clean, hard plastic erasers are best. Use a typist's eraser as the last resort as it will roughen the paper and make subsequent blending impossible. For very localized corrections, an eraser shield will prove very useful.

Making your mark

The scale of the work is an important consideration; do not attempt anything too big as the quality of the mark may lack interest and appear very mechanical. The incisiveness and range of the pencil is best exploited on a small, intimate scale. Keep in mind the capacity of the pencils for overglazing and for hatching one colour over another allowing the colour beneath to show through.

To lay a large, flat area smoothly is one of the most difficult techniques, as the slightest variation in pressure will introduce a change of tone. This is best done using a long, well-blunted point to the pencil. To obtain a dark, even area build up the colour in several flat layers. Laying light colours over dark is possible, but heavy pressure is needed and control is difficult in small areas. A crisp, hard

Above: *The first stage of this landscape concerned the drawing of the composition, when a light tint of colour was given to each area. In the second stage, detail was applied by overlaying colours – "glazing" – until the desired tone and modelling was achieved.*

Right: *To convey the effect of sunlight on the patterned deck chairs, the composition was carefully considered and strong colours were built up solidly alongside one another and very rarely glazed, except where the range of colour needed to be extended.*

edge to an area of colour is easily achieved by covering the edge of the area with a strip of thin paper and shading over onto it.

With the wide range of hues available, and the many variations of tone, one can build up subtle gradations in colour, or create abrupt changes in tone and colour, resulting in a very lively picture. A lesson in how to do this successfully can be learned by rendering a favourite painting in coloured pencil, trying to match the tones and colours.

Portraits and landscapes

For portrait sketches include flesh colour, pink, crimson, red, cobalt blue, cadmium yellow, dark blue, and purple. Begin by sketching in the proportions of the face; this underdrawing will finally disappear under the warm flesh tones if the initial drawing is kept light. Colour the area of the face with the flesh-coloured pencil and add modelling with the red, yellow, and blue. Remember that cool col-ours, such as blues, greens, and purples, are often found in shadows, while warm colours, such as reds and yellows, are found in lighted areas.

In landscape sketching, use predominantly blues and greens, plus two types of red and cadmium yellow. Draw out the proportions as before and cover the whole area with what you see as the predominant colours in the scene. This is then gradually modified by working with the other colours.

Pastels

Pastels are pure pigment held together with the minimum of binding material. Fine, soft pastels are made by British, French, Dutch, and American firms.

They are graded and priced according to the pigment used.

Blending pastels

Although the colours can certainly be blended, not more than three colours can be mixed together before the brilliance of the colour goes. This means that artists working in pastels tend to extend their number of colours so that undue blending is unnecessary. Fortunately, there is an immense range of beautiful colours available.

There are two methods of blending. One is physical, actually welding colours together on the paper, the other is optical, when the blending is done by the eye as it reads colours in close proximity.

Above: *A selection of pastels, drawn across two tones of paper, demonstrating how a colour is modified by the background colour. As is apparent, pastel cannot be easily applied in a tidy and mechanical fashion.*

Right: *Blending can be achieved by a moderate amount of rubbing or smoothing together of colours, or, in a more sophisticated way, allowing strokes of colours on different layers to break through, forming optical blending.*

Opposite: *This drawing uses both techniques; blending is evident in the area of shadow under the heads of the fishes while the sheen of the scales is conveyed by the use of broken flecks of colour. The eyes and wrapping paper are straight application of colour.*

Surfaces

It is helpful to begin using pastels on a toned surface, such as Grey Bogus paper. Brown wrapping paper and construction paper are also useful.

A close look at many of Lautrec's pastels reveals the brilliant incorporation of the background colour into the picture. Although, as with watercolours, drawing with pastels on a rough-surfaced paper gives a brilliance to the medium, it is extremely extravagant of materials, acting on the pastels almost like a grater on cheese. The pace of the drawing on very rough papers is slowed down by the sheer effort of building up enough pigment to give density.

First attempts

The medium demands certain sympathetic and intelligently selected motifs to bring out its best characteristics; speed, beautiful colour, and texture.

Degas, another master of pastel, is well worth close study. His method was to build up form in a series of layers, each one fixed, using immensely confident and informed strokes to convey tone, texture, light, and form. The genius of Degas and Lautrec lay in their ability to retain the bigness of the medium and yet convey the most subtle and intimate detail. Begin with a motif which lends itself to simplification. This does not mean that the motif cannot be trees, flowers, etc; but try to convey mass in your first efforts. The medium should not be used like a thick pencil. Motifs which contain lettering, fine detail such as small patterns on clothing, linear detail, and small natural form should be either avoided when selecting a subject, or ignored or simplified when working on the motif.

Although your first attempts will probably be crude, with experience you will learn when to rub or blend together, when to exploit the effect of separate strokes, when to leave a solid colour area and where a flick of colour could be placed most

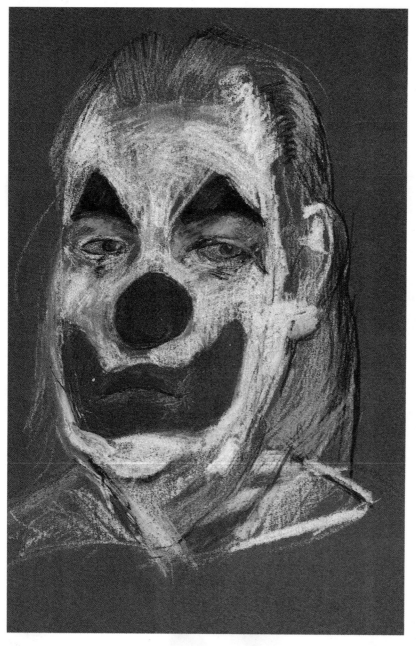

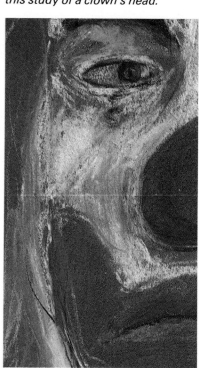

Othello crayons, although not as solid in body colour as traditional pastels, can be sharpened and used to convey quite fine detail, as seen in this study of a clown's head.

effectively. When the drawing is complete, decide whether to fix the pastel or not. Fixing, while stabilizing the powder, also acts as a coagulant and sometimes stains. By applying fixative too heavily, the tones of the work can be changed instantly and irrevocably and spots of fixative which will not evaporate will be clearly visible. The lightest of deposits, applied with a mouth diffuser, rather than an aerosol, is recommended. Apply three coats at ten-minute intervals. Alternatively, protect the work with tissue and frame.

Inevitably, pastels break into smaller and smaller pieces in use, the paper sleeves no longer protect them, and they offset on one another. The contents of a box can become a collection of mud-coloured fragments. A stroke on the side of the paper reveals the former brilliance, but only periodic cleaning with a soft cloth or keeping similar hues together in separate boxes can overcome this.

Pastel need not be a painstaking medium to use. This figure study captures the essentials of the model while retaining a bigness and directness in the drawing.

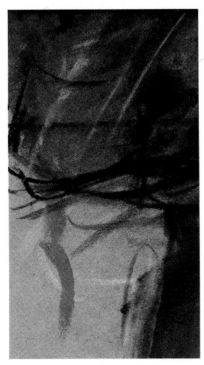

Pen and ink

The most widely used drawing ink is waterproof black, traditionally called India ink. It is excellent for reproduction and allows mistakes to be whited out. It also tolerates fluids which may inadvertently be spilled on it: Its main drawbacks are a tendency to become less viscous as the bottle is increasingly exposed to air, and terrific staining power – it is practically impossible to remove from clothes or paper.

A wide variety of brands is available, from American, British, and German manufacturers. Each brand has a slightly different viscosity and denseness. Experiment with several to find out which one suits your particular way of drawing. Use non-waterproof ink if you wish to reactivate the line

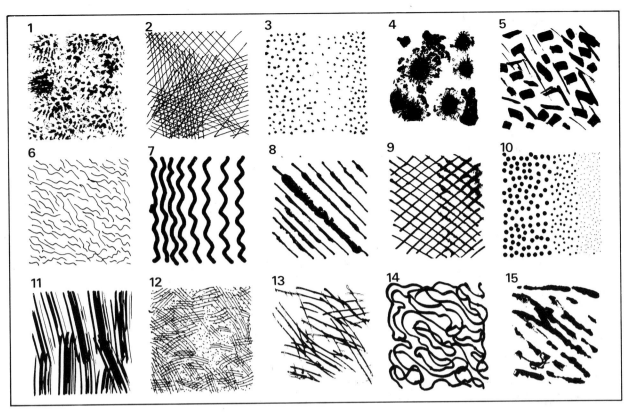

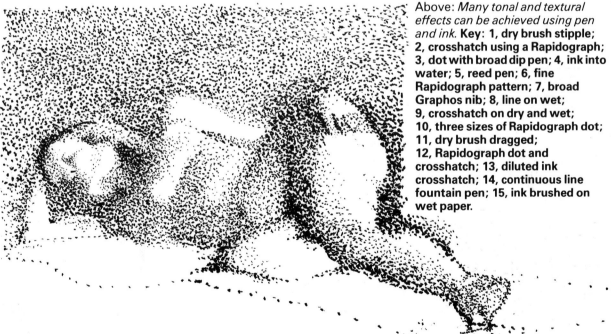

Above: *Many tonal and textural effects can be achieved using pen and ink.* **Key: 1, dry brush stipple; 2, crosshatch using a Rapidograph; 3, dot with broad dip pen; 4, ink into water; 5, reed pen; 6, fine Rapidograph pattern; 7, broad Graphos nib; 8, line on wet; 9, crosshatch on dry and wet; 10, three sizes of Rapidograph dot; 11, dry brush dragged; 12, Rapidograph dot and crosshatch; 13, diluted ink crosshatch; 14, continuous line fountain pen; 15, ink brushed on wet paper.**

Opposite above: *There is a very wide range of pens available to the artist, from the finest steel nibs to calligraphic nibs.*

Left: *Using a fountain pen, this river boat scene was completed in a short period of sustained drawing, without any initial pencil work.*

Above: *The use of the dot technique in pen drawing is slow – tone must be carefully observed and the distribution of the dots controlled to convey contour, form and tone. An initial pencil underdrawing will help when assessing the correct distribution of the dots, which should be built up gradually.*

A straightforward sketch using a dip pen. Tone has been conveyed by crosshatching but the drawing retains an open quality.

for tonal and decorative effect. A range of coloured inks is also available. The colours tend to be harsh, but all inks can be diluted and modified with purified water, which is recommended because it is free from basic impurities present in local water supplies and the colours retain their freshness.

Tools and surfaces

Practically any smooth, non-greasy surface – paper, board, or acetate – is suitable for drawing on. The surface need not be impervious or hard, and there is usually no need to stretch the paper.

Any tool that will convey the ink can be used, depending upon your patience and curiosity. Pens and brushes are the most popular tools. Do not habitually use your best sable brushes for ink, as drawing ink will eventually destroy their whip. Brushes must be thoroughly cleaned in soapy water immediately after use, working the soap well in toward the ferrule to remove all traces of ink.

Dip pens

These are the most simple and direct of pens. A wide range of inexpensive steel nibs and holders are available. Remove the slight greasiness from a new nib by quickly passing it through a gentle flame (prolonged heat will ruin the temper of the nib). It takes some hours of drawing to break in a new nib. A slight build-up of ink on the nib is quite acceptable, though too much will impair its flexibility. Nibs can be scraped clean with a knife, though this may roughen and damage them – time for a new one.

Quill and reed pens have sensitivity and pliability, and were used by masters like Rembrandt

and Van Gogh. Reed pens are still available but quill pens, which require lengthy and highly skilled preparation, are now very rare.

Reservoir pens

Popular and relatively new pens for ink drawing are the Rapidograph and its variants. These tools are designed for engineering and architectural drawing use, and give a continuous flow of ink due to a generous reservoir and specially designed valve system. A variety of expensive monoline nibs, ranging from 0.1mm to 2mm in width, are obtainable. The uniform line they give can be used effectively, though their inflexibility does impose a decorative bias on the drawing. The nibs always remain hard and mechanical in feeling. A

special range of inks, black and some colours, is used.

Ancillary materials

Useful extras when working in pen and ink include blotting paper, rags, and porcelain mixing palettes. Ink stains are almost indelible so do not use your watercolour box lid to hold ink. Keep a spare bottle or two of ink handy.

Drawing on site

Confidence is essential when drawing on site with pen and ink. Nervousness and impatience are transmitted very obviously when working in a medium as unequivocal as black line. Drawing out the motif carefully with a pencil as a guide

Drawing directly with a medium size oil painting brush results in a powerful and decorative study.

should be dispensed with as soon as possible, as it leads to lifeless drawing and will stifle the enjoyment which increases as your confidence grows.

Pen technique can consist of short staccato strokes, mainly in one direction, to build up the form, or be used in a very open technique. When drawing subjects which move, continue drawing despite the inevitable inaccuracies which occur. A degree of excitement will be conveyed if you remain with the motif and keep drawing.

One small factor which can prove a major irritant is the level of ink in the bottle dropping to a point where the nib constantly needs replenishing. Keep the bottle topped up. Buy a large bottle and fill your small bottles before the day's outing. While a medium deposit of ink will dry on the paper quite rapidly, very heavy deposits can take several hours to dry out completely because of the lacquer content.

Working with coloured inks

The brilliance of coloured ink is enhanced by using a good-quality white, smooth paper or even one of the lighter-weight watercolour papers. The paper should be stretched if you intend using wash. Inks can be used in

exactly the same way as watercolours. Distilled water is recommended for easy flow and to lessen a tendency to streakiness. However, any wash which is allowed to dry before completion will leave a hard edge, as ink cannot be reactivated like watercolour. Underpainting in bright colours is very difficult to subdue as subsequent layers of colour tend to give a dirty or very crude effect.

Use as few colours as possible when sketching with inks to avoid a tendency to garishness. Here, three colours and black were used.

Oil painting

Oil paints have a quality and flexibility of handling which, when well used, cannot be rivalled by any other medium, even the recently developed acrylic paints.

Painting mediums

Oil paint consists of dry pigment powder held in suspension by a drying vegetable oil that acts as a binder. A painting medium is used to make the paint easier to apply and also to thin down its consistency.

Many ready-made mediums are available, each having its own use and application. The most common is a mixture of linseed oil and turpentine, but it does have the disadvantage of being slow-drying. Mediums that contain varnish, stand oil, or beeswax overcome this problem and will help to prevent the paint dripping when heavily thinned. Driers are available to shorten the drying time, but they should be used with care as too high a proportion will impair the paint surface.

When choosing mediums, consider the finish required: for a shiny finish, use a varnish medium, and for a matt finish one that contains beeswax.

Dilutents or solvents like turpentine and mineral spirits, which are used for cleaning brushes and palettes, can also be mixed with mediums for further thinning. When used on their own, the binding power of the oil paint is impaired, and the paint surface is liable to crack.

Brushes

It is important to have a good selection of hog hair and sable brushes. Sable brushes give a smoother, softer stroke than hog hair and are usually kept for fine work and detail. Various synthetic brushes are also available.

Most brushes come in a variety of shapes: bright, flat, round, and filbert. Brights have short bristles, and are used for applying thick, creamy paint. Flats are useful for broad and direct work, rounds for small areas and for applying heavily thinned paint. Filberts make shaped, tapering marks.

All come in a range of sizes, usually from 1 (the smallest) up to 12, but larger sizes are available. A good working selection of brushes would include several sizes of each of the basic shapes.

Right: *Stretching and priming a canvas; stretcher pieces are slotted together to form a rectangle of the proportions required. Check the corners are square by measuring the diagonals. Fold the canvas round the sides of the stretchers and using a staple gun, secure the canvas to the centre of the outside edges.*

There are many methods of preparing absorbent surfaces to receive oil paints. A traditional method is to apply three coats of size to the surface – following the manufacturer's instructions – and follow by two coats of white canvas primer, allowing twenty four hours drying time between each coat.

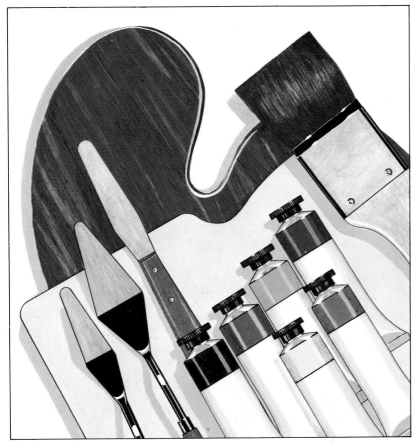

Brushes should be carefully looked after, removing paint with mineral spirits or turpentine, and then washing them with soap and water. Do not leave brushes standing in solvent for any length of time.

Palettes and other tools

Palette knives are useful for mixing paints and cleaning the palette, and can also be used as painting knives for applying thick paint directly to the canvas.

A shaped, wooden palette is useful, but any non-absorbent surface such as glass or plastic will do the job.

Palette cups – small open cans for holding oil and turpentine – are convenient, as they can be clipped to hand-held palettes, but any suitable container can be used.

A large range of easels is available, from large, studio ones to the small sketching variety. The choice will depend on your requirements.

Surfaces

The most widely used painting surface or support for oil paint is canvas. This material is ideal when stretched and primed with a suitable ground. Wood, ply-

Opposite: *Try a wide variety of shapes and sizes of brush before you decide on the particular shape or quality of brush which suits you best. It is a mistake to try to economise by using only two or three.*

Above: *The traditional wood palette has a useful mid-tone to help evaluate the colours. A varnishing brush should be large, and painting knives with their delicate temper are necessary for applying paint in the more detailed passages.*

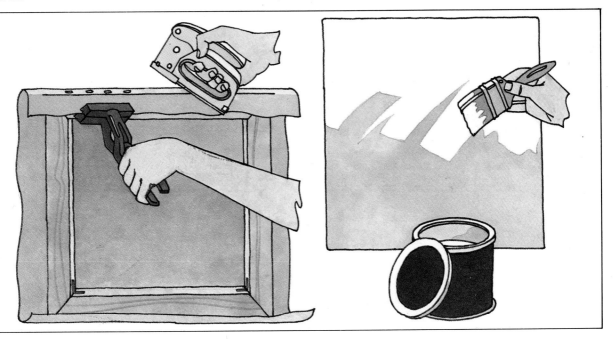

wood, metal, cardboard, and paper are alternatives, but require careful preparation.

The simplest but most expensive way of obtaining a canvas is to buy one ready stretched and primed. Commercially prepared boards which have a simulated canvas surface are also available. Many artists prefer to prepare their own supports, buying the linen, cotton, and hessian canvas and stretching and priming it themselves. Linen is the best support, but a good quality cotton is almost as good. Hessian is very coarse and requires a lot of priming. The shiny surface of hardboard provides an alternative to canvas, but it must be battened and sized to prevent warping.

Both oil- and acrylic-based primers are available for use with oil paints. The support must be given a coat of glue size solution before an oil-based primer is used. The primer should be applied in two thin coats, as one thick coat may crack and leave an uneven, shiny surface.

Using oil paints

Oil paint is a highly flexible medium and, while all painters develop their own approach to it, some understanding of its basic uses and capabilities is important when starting.

Right: Three ways of applying oil paint: from top to bottom; scumbling is opaque paint applied over another layer in an irregular way; glazes are created by laying thin coats of paint, diluted with a suitable medium, over a painted surface; stippling is useful for producing broken areas of colour. Apply the paint in dots or short strokes.

The one rule for oils is to use "fat over lean", which means that the oil content of the medium is increased with each layer of paint. This will stop the surface cracking as the paint begins to dry.

Oils can be used for carefully planned works that are built up layer by layer, or in a very direct and spontaneous manner, often using thick, impasto paint to express the immediacy and feel of a subject. Impasto is paint mixed with a resinous medium or gel, and applied with a brush or knife. This creates a surface texture, and the expressive quality of the brush strokes can be used to build up form and movement within a composition.

Painting "wet into wet" is the technique of applying a colour on top of another that is still wet so that the colours blend or run into each other. This technique is particularly useful in very direct and immediate forms of painting.

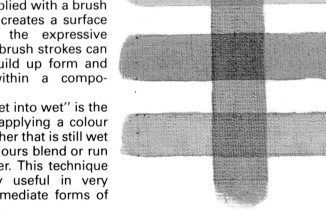

Some surfaces suitable for oil painting are, left to right; Daler board, primed hardboard, canvas-surfaced board, linen canvas.

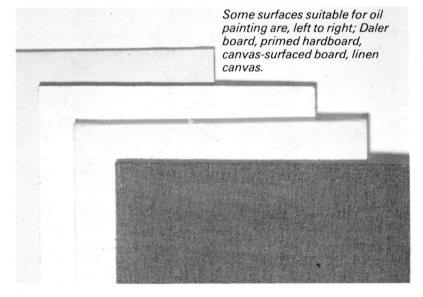

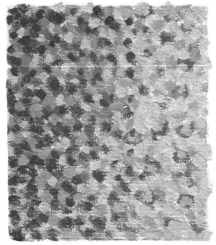

Above: *While oil paint comes in a wide range of colours, a limited palette can be used to good effect as can be seen in this still-life. The colours used were; titanium white, French ultramarine, sap green, cadmium yellow, yellow ochre, vermillion and alizarin crimson.*

Right: *Colour is a very personal matter, but a useful palette for the beginner would include (reading clockwise); titanium white, lemon yellow, yellow ochre, cadmium red, light red, rose madder, burnt umber, burnt sienna, cobalt blue and French ultramarine. Greens, like oranges and purples, are not essential as they can be mixed, though viridian green and terre verte are particularly useful.*

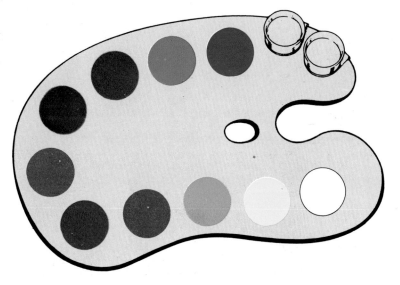

Sketching in oils

It is important when working outside to have all your equipment well organized. A lightweight, collapsable sketching easel and a stool are important pieces of equipment, especially when working in places where a good deal of carrying and travelling are involved.

Always check that you have everything you need before setting out, and make sure that there is sufficient paint in the tubes for the work that is planned.

Mediums and solvents should be in leakproof containers and the palette should be light and easy to hold.

Sketching technique

The aim of sketching in oils should be to capture the essence of a particular scene or mo-ment. When making landscape sketches, a direct or alla prima method of painting is usually employed. With this approach a painting is completed in a single session, using opaque colours. The paint is applied freely with a brush or knife capturing the freshness of colour and feeling of a place.

It requires confidence because the artist must work quickly and boldly and must not be afraid to change passages in the picture either by overpainting or scraping off.

Sketches can be used as working drawings for studio paintings, but these often lack the life and vitality of the initial statement.

In the sketch above, the paint was applied with no underpainting or drawing. Areas of colour were applied directly, the dark colours and tones being put down first, and worked into

Above: *This picture contains many of the elements normally encountered on a day's landscape sketching. A selection of sable brushes – none larger than size 8 – was used, because of the fine detail of the foliage and the distances.*

Opposite: *The first stage shows a quick but thorough record of the main elements of the scene. Speed was necessary as storm clouds threatened rain. The oil content was kept low to speed drying. As the work progressed, the trees on the right were removed, allowing a more dramatic rendering of the wooden gates against the sky.*

while still wet. Mistakes can be wiped or scraped out.

The painting of lock gates on the facing page (top) was stopped after one hour. In the next stage this initial statement has been worked up and refined, although all the important elements were already established.

Acrylics

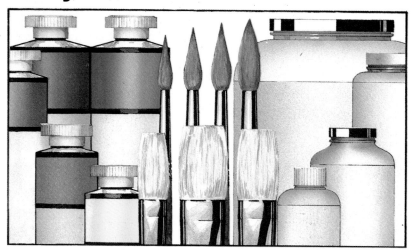

Acrylics are a recent innovation developed originally for large, exterior murals. They are extremely flexible and can be used in a variety of ways. Made from pigment bound in a synthetic resin, the paint can be thinned with water and dries to form a waterproof layer. Speed in drying makes acrylic a very convenient medium.

The colour range is similar to oils, but some of the names are different because new synthetic dyes and pigments have been developed.

They can be applied to virtually any dry, oil-free surface. Canvas can be used unprimed, or with a ground of acrylic primer. Brushes and equipment are the same as for oils. Brushes should be thoroughly cleaned with soap and water immediately after use to prevent hardening.

Acrylic mediums

The mediums for use with acrylics are cloudy or milky in the bottle, becoming transparent when dry. The combination of mediums and acrylics can produce many interesting effects.

There are gloss and matt mediums for both general painting and glazing and a gel medium for impasto work. A thick modelling paste is also

Above: *A range of the most useful brush sizes and types of acrylics available.*

Right: *Two beach cabins made an ideal subject for acrylics. The sand in the foreground and at the side of the cabins was rendered using a dry brush and small quantities of paint, dragged across the surface. Details of the weathered woodwork were added using the smallest sizes of brushes.*

available. For very thick impasto, gel or modelling paste is mixed with a small amount of colour. Paints can be used with water alone in a similar technique to that employed for watercolours. However, the addition of at least a drop of

Left: *Acrylics can be applied in many ways. From left to right: very dilute "watercolour" wash technique; impasto using a palette knife; impasto using a brush; glazing over impasto using a diluted top coat.*

medium will help the paint to flow more easily, and will give greater depth and body to washes. An acrylic retarder can be used to slow the drying time and painting "wet into wet" is made easier by its use.

Using acrylic paint

While acrylics are frequently employed using a watercolour technique and the traditional oil-painting techniques of building up a picture by underpainting and overglazing, they do lend themselves naturally to a direct approach.

However, before starting to paint with acrylics, a certain amount of planning is necessary. It is important to consider the effects you wish to achieve. These can range from the illustrative considerations of the subject matter (what it is, and what is happening) to the impressionistic and expressive qualities of light and colour, movement and feeling.

While it is important to be flexible and keep an open mind on the subject so that new ideas can be seen and exploited as the work progresses, remember that acrylics do not allow quite the same scope as oils. Unlike oils, which can still be moved about, scraped, or wiped off some time after application, acrylics leave little time for deliberation or change once they have been laid down. Brush marks dry precisely as they are made, and the tactile or surface quality of the paint should be considered in the overall plan of the composition.

1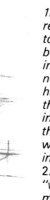

1. With a fine brush, the point relationship technique is first used to establish the crucial relationships between the pianist and his instrument. Normally it would be necessary to make many studies of hands and postures before starting the work, but due to the inconvenience this would cause the pianist, photographic reference was used as additional information.
2. Basic local colour is applied in a "watercolour" technique using medium size brushes.
3. The general tonal areas of the subject become more defined and structural and specific details of the stool and piano are added. The paint is used more heavily to convey solidity and mass in the main elements.
4. In the final stage, the tones and colours are adjusted and the positions of the hands and feet are thoroughly worked out. Some of the original watercolour effect is retained as being adequate to explain the qualities of the wood and some shadow areas. For the more crucial areas of the hands and face, a fine brush was used and the modelling carefully built up using thin washes.

Gouache

Gouache colours are superb for painting on a small, intimate scale. They are water-based and come in a wide range of colours. They can be used as a transparent wash or opaquely to dry as flat colour. They can also be used in a broader fashion to give a painterly texture. Their beauty lies in their versatility, and this should be exploited to the full, creating in a single painting a variety of surfaces both transparent and opaque.

Any type of paper can be used for gouache, as long as it is stretched or is thick enough not to buckle.

Left: *A middle range of soft brushes is most useful for gouache.*

Below: *Three examples of gouache application: left, glazing; centre, impasto; right, free brushwork.*

Choosing paints

Gouache colours are available in two qualities. The cheaper range of colours, usually called poster paints, are sold in pots of varying sizes and can be bought singly or in sets of six, eight, or twelve basic colours.

The more expensive and extensive range are called Designer's Gouache and are available in tubes. The permanence of the colour is rated by a star or alphabet system. The brilliance and saturation of the colours is achieved by a heavy and not too finely ground pigment content, combined with a slight lowering of the amount of binding medium.

Colours for the palette

Use a clean, plastic palette, preferably white, so that the small quantities of colour can be seen clearly and correctly against it.

Above: *Using the medium in a controlled and precise way, the rich, low-key harmonies of this picture demonstrate the wide possibilities of gouache, its use to convey solid, opaque form and texture together with a delicate, watercolour-like atmosphere.*

Below: *Gouache can also be used in a more vigorous way to convey the mood and atmosphere of a less intimate motif. Opaque areas in the sky are balanced against a wash treatment of the trees and river. The whole painting will dry quickly at its different levels.*

An expressive picture can result from using gouache in a direct way. In stage one the areas are defined and underlying colour is applied with a large brush using heavily diluted paint. In stage two a build up of tone and colour takes place. The dark area of the buildings and trees are applied as broad masses, over which lighter detailing will take place. The last stage is built up by a confident multiplicity of strokes, with no need for blending.

1

3

2

A suggested range of colours would include the following; red ochre, flame red, alizarin crimson, cadmium yellow, lemon yellow, chromium oxide (green), sap green, cobalt blue, Prussian blue, and white.

There are two types of white in gouache, and they should be selected with the desired effect in mind. Permanent white has a high pigment content and covers well, though it does make colours somewhat chalky. Zinc white has a low pigment con-tent, is more transparent, and is useful when glazing one colour over another. A black can be mixed using roughly equal quantities of Indian red and Prussian blue.

Gouache colours tend to crack if applied too thickly, but this can be prevented by using a pro-prietary acrylizing or plasticizing medium. They also have a ten-dency to dry slightly darker than when wet in the case of light colours, and slightly lighter in the case of dark ones, though this will not disturb any but the most exacting colourist.

Brushes

A selection of soft brushes will be required, either of sable or the new nylon equivalents. Sable and ox hair mixture brushes can also be used. Brushes consisting of pure ox or squirrel hair tend to be less springy than the sable or nylon, and therefore not quite as easy to control.

Samuel Marshall.

A useful selection of brushes to begin with would include: a ¾-inch flat brush for covering large areas; a size 4 and a size 6 round brush for covering smaller areas and for most of the modelling (the round brushes can be brought to a fine point for quite detailed work); a size 1 brush for the most finely detailed work.

This selection can later be supplemented with a personal choice from the large variety of brushes available. All brushes will repay careful treatment by extended life and greater consistency. Never allow paint to dry on the bristles and do not leave brushes standing in water for long periods. After use, rinse thoroughly, removing excess water and shaping to a point.

Basic painting method

Draw out your composition either in pencil or in a very dilute blue. Flood the first colours on with water in a generous wash to cover the entire composition. From this you can build up the colours more opaquely. If you are covering a large area with one colour, mix sufficient colour to cover it in one go. Otherwise you will have the problem of matching the colour, which can be difficult. Use the brush that is appropriate for the job; do not try to cover large areas with a small brush. Practise applying the paint both opaquely and as a transparent wash until you have mastered the techniques.

Watercolour

Much of today's great water-colour tradition stems from the paintings of the masters of the eighteenth and nineteenth centuries, whose work set a standard of technical virtuosity and artistic sensibility by which all subsequent work in the medium has been measured.

Paints

Watercolour is pure pigment, finely ground from various natural mineral and vegetable substances, bound with glycerine. It is sold in pans or half pans or in two different sizes of tubes. The paint is graded by quality and classified by degree of permanence. Cheaper ranges are available as student quality.

Surfaces

The most usual surface or support for watercolour painting is paper. To obtain the maximum potential from artists' quality watercolours, a rag-based paper should be used.

Paper is manufactured in a wide variety of weights and textures. The heavier the paper, the more expensive it is. A workable range would extend from 90 to 200 pounds. Textures are normally specified in three grades: rough, hot pressed (HP), and cold pressed (CP).

Lighter weight papers should be stretched onto a firm wooden board using packaging tape. A good paper will stand up to a certain amount of rough treatment and hold the colour on the surface, giving optimum freshness and brightness. Good-

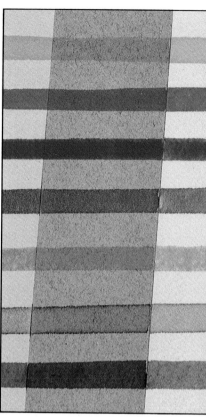

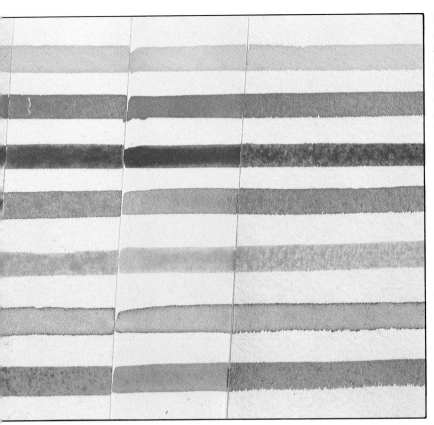

Left: *This chart containing a selection of quality, rag-based papers of different weights and surfaces, demonstrates how colour is affected tonally and texturally by the various surfaces. All papers can be readily obtained from art supply shops. Experiment to see which ones suit your requirements best.*

quality paper is gelatine-sized throughout.

The manufacturer's name or mark can be read by holding the paper up to the light. The side from which it can be read correctly is the right side to use.

Brushes

Brushes should be the best quality that you can afford. Sable has the softness, re-silience, and water-holding qualities necessary for the finest control. Nylon brushes are now widely available and are worth trying. Applying broad washes

Opposite: *Good quality brushes are important when using watercolour, sometimes combined with gouache or inks.*

Right: *By covering each of the halves of the head in turn the techniques used to achieve the finished image can be seen. Although the glazes are used very thinly on the right they immediately begin to model the form and place the main features. Further controlled glazes complete the substance and colour of the head.*

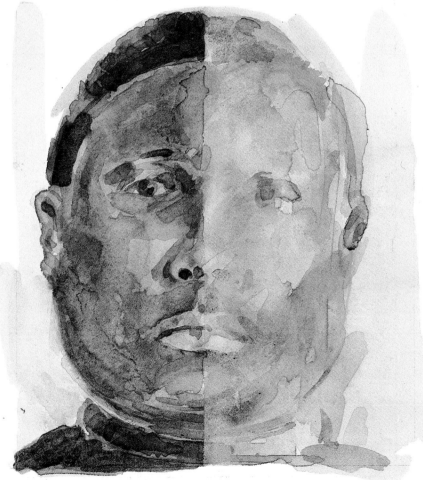

calls for a large, pliable brush, shape being of personal preference. Flat, round, or square brushes are available made of sable, ox, or squirrel hair.

Painting techniques

The techniques of applying the paint to the chosen surface call for a personal choice. Nolde, Cotman, De Wint, Cézanne, Segonzac, all masters of watercolours, used techniques of very differing character, ranging from highly organized thin washes built up in glazes to a solid, almost impasto, use of the medium. The small, mosaic-like areas of a Prendergast contrast with the large calm areas of a De Wint.

In watercolour painting the luminosity and purity of the colours are exploited by allowing the natural white of the paper to strike through even the darkest tones. If using a tinted paper, then any whites or luminous areas such as clouds are best conveyed by the use of diluted gouache colour. This is a wholly acceptable introduction; Turner and many of his contemporaries had no qualms about using gouache and watercolour together.

Colours appear to be fresher when used on CP or rough paper as the texture of the paper

Right: *Stretching paper for watercolour; tear or cut four strips of ¾-inch packaging tape slightly longer than the sides of the board. Tear or cut paper to size about 1½-inches smaller all around than the board. Read the watermark on the paper to determine which is the right side and mark one corner.*

Submerge the paper in water, being careful not to crease it and thus weaken the fibres. Leave to soak for five to fifteen minutes, depending on the weight of the paper. The heavier the paper, the longer it should be soaked. Lift out carefully and allow the water to run from one corner until the flow becomes a slow drip. Place the paper squarely on the board, marked side uppermost, and with a dampened hand smooth all air bubbles out to the edges. Dampen packaging tape sparingly – too much water causes it to curl and washes off the gum – and burnish down, half on the paper, half on the board. Gently remove surplus water from the paper with a tissue, giving special attention to areas where packaging tape and paper meet. Leave flat to dry naturally.

A fluid technique displays to good advantage the freshness and directness of watercolours. A combination of wet into wet and overglazing enables broad masses as well as the more detailed parts to be handled quickly and easily. No preliminary underdrawing was done as this would have impaired the spontaneity of the work. The paper used had a hard finish which kept the colour on the surface and helped to retain its brilliance.

causes a minute breakdown of the wash, giving a natural sparkle of light and dark tones to the painting.

HP paper is valuable for use with a technique which employs small overlapping areas, strictly controlled, as the means of building up form and atmosphere. Cozens, Cézanne, or Prendergast could be studied as exponents of this technique.

To some degree, the motif you are painting will determine your handling and technique, so be flexible in your approach. A seascape will obviously demand a quicker, broader, and therefore more fluid treatment than a still life.

A watercolour can soon show the effects of sluggish or tentative handling, and overworking is another factor which immediately begins to obscure the paper's great contribution of translucency. Although watercolour can be applied in an impastolike manner, it is worth remembering that the finest work shows fluidity, atmosphere, and spontaneity.

Painting on location

Equipment for watercolour painting should include the following: stretched paper (either on a frame or drawing board) or a good quality watercolour block; a light but sturdy easel and a folding stool; a good range of artists' quality colours with extra pens or tubes of the colours you use most; a selection of brushes; a waterproof satchel and box containing blotting paper, a sharp knife (for scratching out highlights), a small natural sponge, a cloth or rag, cottonwool buds (for lifting out highlights), pencils, an eraser, and one or two mediums if you like them. Oxgall is always useful, but you will soon find what suits you best. Finally, you will need large, stable, plastic containers to hold clean water.

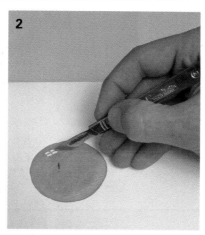

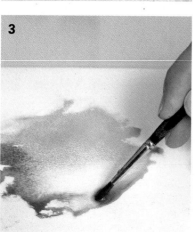

Above: *Direct but carefully considered brush work was used in this still-life of an old boat. The boat's supports have been left uncompleted to show how both light and dark tones may be the starting point for depicting objects. No preliminary drawing was made, but working in the centre of the large sheet of paper ensured that the motif would safely fit. A light wash was quickly laid over the white paper before work began, to subdue the glare on a sunny day.*

Left: *Watercolour can take many forms and can be altered by technical devices once applied. The photographs show: lifting broad highlights (figure 1); scratching detailed highlights (figure 2); painting slowly and deliberately wet into wet (figure 3); painting quickly wet into wet, giving a diffuse line effect (figure 4).*

Opposite: *Using a limited number of low-key colours, small overlapping areas of colour were used to convey the masonry and fragmented tones of the motif. The overall use of warm colour has been offset by carefully placed, cool (blue) notes to avoid a monochromatic effect.*

47

1

The subject of this step-by-step watercolour was carefully chosen, with the village in the middle distance, and the interesting geometric shapes of the buildings contrasting well with the gentle slopes of the tree-clad valley. The diagonal line of the fence breaks up the foreground.

1.   A carefully considered pencil drawing was made using an HB pencil on a medium weight paper with a soft surface, to indicate the angles of the roofs and walls of the buildings. Some of the main tonal areas were lightly shaded in as an aid to assessing the composition of the motif. The colour of the sky was lightly washed in.

2

2.   In the second stage the pencil drawing was slightly erased, and the shaded areas were completely removed. The tints of the foliage and the pale tones of the buildings and fence were washed in using a size 5 sable brush. The importance of the areas of snow as a strong design factor in the picture became immediately apparent. No further work was done on the sky at this stage.

3.   Mid tones were now added to the buildings to convey the solidity of the forms, and to the fence. A darker tone was placed in the windows and doorway to give depth. The sky received additional layers of colour. Shadow areas were added across the snow. Some foliage and a build up of the pattern formed by the branches of the trees were indicated. Specific detailing of foliage and stonework, slates, etc. is not added until the overall tones in the painting are correctly balanced. Heavy tones can upset this balance and require correction. This can be time-consuming, particularly in cold weather, as drying times are prolonged in low temperatures.

4.   The sky was completed, and when dry, the pattern of fine branches was added, using small brushes. The tones of the branches should be carefully evaluated and indicated, without reworking, as it is not easy to remove a mistake at this stage. The patterns of stonework and slates, the texture of the wooden fence, and the blades of grass in the foregound were the finishing touches.

Mixed media

Mixed media is the use of different paint media together. The water-based paints such as acrylic, gouache, watercolour, and even pencil, crayon, and pastel, can be used effectively in the same painting. The basic rule for using water-based and oil-based media in the same painting is to apply the water-based media first, overlaid by the oil paint, since the water-based paint will not adhere to the oil.

Pastels in particular are ideal to mix with other media, especially watercolour, used either as a base or an overlay. Degas experimented widely with pastel, using it with charcoal and even over a thin application of oil paint and turpentine.

Collage

The sheer weight and diversity of photographic and printed matter now existing has produced a variety of new techniques available for artistic expression.

Collage is probably the most straightforward of these techniques. It consists of using coloured materials to create an image or picture. There is no real limitation to the materials used; however, it must be possible for them to be stuck on a support, and for this reason weight is of prime importance. The most useful materials are coloured cloths and papers, the latter often being taken from glossy magazines and chosen for their colours and textures.

A similar process was used to great effect by Matisse in his later years, using paper coloured with gouache and subsequently cut to shape. The technique allows a diversity of handling; the paper can be cut or torn,

since music is an abstract art which is expressive without being illustrative of the every-day world, the same could be true of painting.

They found a parallel to every aspect of music; like it, painting deals with colour, tone, pitch, harmony, discord, point, and counterpoint.

Marc Rothko, the American abstract expressionist painter, dealt with tone in an abstract and atmospheric way. He paint-ed fields of very dark colours onto canvases, often of massive proportions. During the more mature period of his work these paintings became dark, some-times almost black. On top of the fields he painted atmospheric and diffused rectangles, causing them to float in the dark space of the canvas without any attempt at elaborate composition. The tones of the rectangles he would alter only very slightly from the background tone, thus pro-ducing an extraordinary effect of atmospheres suspended and oscillating in space.

Try experimenting yourself with this use of tone, varying the colours but keeping the same tonal value, that is to say, the same grade of lightness or dark-ness of colour.

Painters like Robert Mother-well used dark organic shapes painted with energetic, physical marks. Motherwell's paintings also have what might be called syncopated rhythm, because the bold compositions often set up regular shapes, sometimes almost symmetrical yet slightly off-beat by virtue of the fact that the shapes are altered by chance elements as is often the case in natural organic forms. Attempt to enhance your sense of rhythm by taking a shape and practising painting it over and over again, examining and mod-ifying it each time in different ways. This exercise is invaluable for increasing your powers of perception.

The archetypal action painter, Jackson Pollock, dealt with rhythm and tone in the most in-teresting and unexpected ways. He dripped and trailed paint across the surface of his canvases in rhythmic patterns, allowing the threads of paint to interweave across one another, creating a fine mesh of lines. He thereby produced an illusion of a vast complexity of forms.

The impressionistic effects of light and atmosphere are mono-chromatically conveyed in Monet's Flood at Giverny. *The shapes of the trees provide a necessary rhythm across the picture.*

Opposite: *Pissarro's painting,* The Côtes des Boeufs at L'Hermitage near Pontoise *combines Impressionist philosophy of light and atmosphere with the traditional norms of form and solidity.*

Above: *This striking composition by Seurat,* Le Bec du Hoc, *shows his interest in the scientific colour theories of the day.*

One only has to follow one of the threads of paint across the canvas to appreciate its rhythmic qualities.

Pollock achieved his effects by intuitive positioning of the splashes of colour and direction of the dripped trails of paint rather than by a preconceived sense of order. The paintings are most effective when carried out on a large scale so that the observer is able to stand close to the canvas and, in doing so, is absorbed by the strands of paint meandering across the fields and splashes of colour. The observer thereby relives the making of the painting.

An impression of colour

The use of colour by painters such as Monet, Pissarro, and Sisley is very interesting. The Impressionist philosophy was that, instead of a change of tone, a change of colour is equally valid. Many of their paintings, particularly those of Monet, are very brightly coloured, almost of a single tone, but with such changes of colour that the canvas almost appears to vibrate with pent-up energy. This theory was taken further by the French Post-Impressionists Bonnard and Vuillard, whose beautiful figure paintings are somewhat difficult to decipher at first because of the unexpected use of pattern, tone, and colour.

Try taking a painting of your own, or one that you admire by one of the masters and rendering it in a scheme of colours without altering the tones. This will give you a feeling for the difference between tone and colour; it is important to be clear about the distinction.

A contemporary of the Impressionists, Georges Seurat, was also interested in colour. His paintings, however, were constructed more scientifically than those of the Impressionists. The canvases, which were painted during a period of great scientific advance, mirror in their execution the belief in the validity of science as a modern panacea. Seurat applied paint to the canvas as dots or strokes of pure colour. These demonstrated the then new optical theories; the colour being mixed optically by the eye of the observer, as opposed to physically by the artist.

The composition of his paintings was also tightly constructed, obeying the classical rules of aesthetics, based upon the perfect rectangle, and a proportion known as the "Golden Section". The completed paintings, for all their theoretical construction and careful execution, have a life of their own. Some of his landscapes, viewed from a distance, shimmer with light.

Another painter often classed with the Impressionists was Paul Cézanne. Though some of his works correspond to the appearance of Impressionist canvases, his intentions and aspirations were far removed from that area. This is demonstrated by the thickness of the

paint on many of the canvases of his middle period, which were heavily worked in an attempt to construct the subject on the canvas.

During Cézanne's mature period, he retained the bright colours of the Impressionist palette, while the application of paint became thinner and more precisely controlled.

A problem central to Cézanne's interests consisted of reconstructing the visible world on the canvas in terms of geometric shapes, namely the cube, the sphere, and the cone. In this, he was the precursor of cubism, and his work was later admired and studied by Braque and Picasso, as a starting point from which they produced their cubist paintings.

This is, however, an over-simplification. While geometric shapes can be seen to be the basis used to build the composition on the canvas, it was the construction which was the important factor to the artist.

Cézanne required of his art solidity and durability. He therefore used the transient nature of light to reveal shape and space in the form of planes which either advance or recede on the picture surface.

In the earliest days of abstract painting, colour was the area of major importance for artists such as Wassily Kandinsky. This artist felt that colour had a symbolic association and therefore was a universal language. Kandinsky was a member of a school of painting known as the Blue Rider; the title was taken from the subject of one of Kandinsky's earliest canvases in this style. Their use of colour was based on a considered, though expressive arrangement, sometimes based on things seen, but often stylized into almost abstract shapes.

A contemporary of Kandinsky, Johann Itten, looked upon colour as a seminal subject. He was a theorist who wrote a book in which he discussed the various qualities of colour, for example, discordant colour, when a colour with a normally dark tone is set against a colour of a normally light tone. This type of juxtaposition can often be seen in the paintings of artists such as Kandinsky, Paul Klee, and their contemporaries.

Many artists have found a life's work in the exploration of the subtleties of colour. Your aim as a painter is to discover in your own work the area of study which interests you most; it might be light or form, colour or tone, texture or composition. Any aspect is worthy of study, and, when you have chosen an area, or it has chosen you, see how other artists have used it and where it occurs in nature and your environment and develop it as far as you can. Above all else, be prepared to look at everything with a clear and discerning eye.

Opposite: *In this portrait,* The Gardener, *Cézanne's grasp of colour harmonies is seen to good advantage. The background colours which start with cool blues on the left gradually wrap around and almost envelop the gardener in green organic forms. Little distinction is made between background colours and those used to depict the figure, which closely associates the gardener with his surroundings.*

Right: *This abstract shows interesting juxtapositions and changes of tone and colour.*

LANDSCAPES

Sketching

A sketch is a preliminary, and often unfinished, drawing or painting. Used experimentally, it can help you learn about technique, or as a means of self-expression. As a rough draft for a finished work without detail but with broad outlines, a sketch can suggest ideas or be an enjoyable way of recording observations. It should be approached with confidence as an immediate and spontaneous way of expressing yourself.

Sketches are often enjoyed for their own sake and are preferred by many to more finished work.

Sketching allows freedom to combine pencils with watercolour or pen and ink or both. You can begin with one and work

over with the other. Or you can do two or more drawings of the same subject in different painting and drawing media.

Sketching should attempt to explore the possibilities of a scene, and differs from formal studies in that it will suggest rather than explain what is observed.

A sketch is, therefore, inclined to be a hit-or-miss affair, but therein lies its charm and also its usefulness to the beginner as a method of working. It may be more expendable, but often displays qualities that more finished works lack.

Sketching outdoors plays an important role in understanding landscape and a knowledge of the materials helps to produce good results. Simplicity is the keynote; be prepared for the unexpected by taking a selection of

Opposite top: *The angular lines of the building in the background are contrasted with the natural shape of the trees.*

Opposite bottom: *In this sketch, the mountainous clouds are echoed and amplified by the rolling hills of the terrain beneath.*

Right: *A simple canvas roll can be made easily and cheaply and is invaluable for keeping your materials together.*

materials, even if you have planned your excursion before.

Sketchbooks

Hard-cover sketchbooks are a necessary part of your equipment. They keep your work together, the hard covers provide protection and act as a drawing board. They come in many sizes and many surfaces. Some sketchbooks have a variety of different surfaced papers to allow for many ways of working. Fill your sketchbook consecutively. Do not jump about. Remember to date and

Above: *The mood created by this sketch is one of calm repose.*

annotate sketches with written notes.

Satchels

Sketching materials should be light and portable. It is not always possible to use transport to the best spots and you may have to walk, so it is a good idea to have a strong, light satchel to take pencils, pens, watercolours, brushes, and paper safely and comfortably.

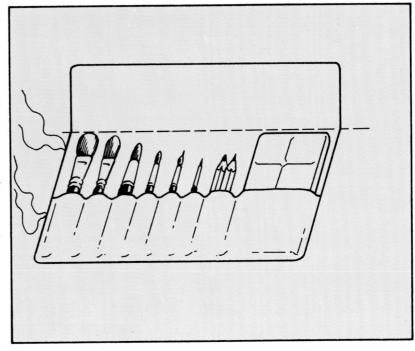

Composition: proportion and balance

Nature does not exist in a rectangle, whereas paintings do. Surfaces are generally rectangular and this means that we need to select and arrange what we see in order to ensure that our paintings are coherent and convincing. For this purpose we need to know something about composition.

There are two basic principles which are involved in the creation of a successful composition: proportion and balance, and rhythm and movement.

Proportion

Surfaces are available in landscape, portrait, or square format. Each shape has a characteristic thrust. In a horizontal rectangle the eye is encouraged to move across, in a vertical it moves up and down. In a square the thrusts are equal, creating a static composition, which is possibly why this format is not often used.

Landscapes, naturally, tend to fit better into horizontal rectangles. Nature, while it is full of variety and vitality, is always in harmony. The proportions are never seen to be equal. A rectangle, on the other hand, can be divided equally or unequally. Equal divisions tend to be static and lack vitality and

unequal ones tend to suggest movement. The "happiest" division which seems to enhance yet harmonize within a rectangle is a division of the rectangle into three parts. They may be equal thirds or unequal, upright or horizontal.

The difficulty with a symmetrical composition is that, though it may work with some kind of subject matter: still life, flower painting, portraits, and townscapes, it rarely works with landscape because it is not dynamic enough. Even the most carefully planned park cannot be symmetrically arranged on the support without looking unreal and therefore unconvincing.

Placing important objects like trees, buildings, farm equipment, gates, immediately in the centre of the painting destroys the visual excitement and is likely to produce boredom.

Proportion is mainly concerned with the way in which you

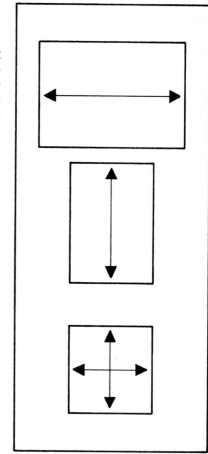

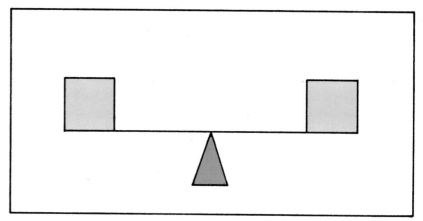

distribute the main areas of your composition.

The distribution of shapes and masses is the function of balance.

Balance

Balance in a composition is concerned with creating a centre of interest or focal point that will not disrupt the unity of the whole, or be overwhelmed by other elements.

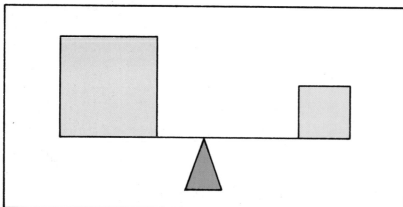

The eye continually moves from one point of interest to another in order to build a complete image in the mind. If points of interest are not properly related they will create an imbalance in the composition which will reduce and make trivial in the painting what was seen as dynamic in the original landscape. This is why most people at some time have taken a photograph of a breathtaking landscape only to be disappointed by the print obtained. The camera does not in itself emphasize a point of interest.

If the relationship of the parts of the composition are of equal visual weight and are symmetrically placed, the result will tend to look static and uninteresting. If, on the other hand, the parts are unequal and are asymmetrically placed, the result will be full of interest, movement, and contrast. It will be seen that asymmetrical compositions will be more suitable for landscape painting than symmetrical ones.

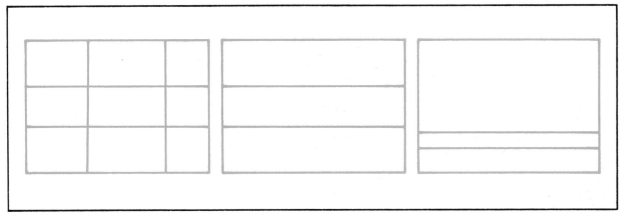

Opposite above: *The format of the paper suggests the visual thrust.*

Opposite below: *In these illustrations, both scales are in equilibrium but the lower one is more dynamic.*

Above: *The "happiest" division of any rectangle is into thirds. The proportions created by the division can vary considerably and the focal point can sit on a line or be encapsulated by them.*

Below: *The format of this painting is based upon the division shown in the illustration above. The focal point of the painting is the fields framed by the trees in the middle distance.*

Composition: rhythm and movement

The composition of any drawing or painting relies on a visual harmony created by the tension of the lines, masses, or colour areas which exert a pull opposed by an equal pull in the opposite direction. The quality of any line, for example, will produce a direction and feel of its own: a smooth, curving line will lead the eye gently along its length and create a soothing effect, while a deeply incised erratic line will evoke tension and drama. It must be remembered that every directional pull has to be balanced, otherwise the observer's eye will be projected off the picture surface. Equilibrium is the essence of composition, but it should be an interesting equilibrium.

Visual movement

It is the rhythm and movement set up in a painting which should cause the eye to roam around the picture and arrive finally and inexorably at the focal point. From here it may well begin the journey again, possibly in a different way, but it should always return. If the eye is allowed to drift across the surface and finds nothing to interest it, there is something wrong with the composition.

The more the observer's eye is allowed to rove about the painting, the more interested it will be and the more it will be prompted

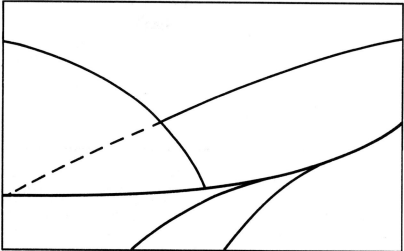

Above and left: *The direction lines of the keyline diagram show the main lines that the eye will follow or be affected by as it scans the painting.*

Opposite right: *The line formed by the pebbles and boulders on the bank leads the eye into the picture.*

Opposite far right: *In this painting the eye tends to rest upon the line of the hill in the foreground and scan across it looking at the view in the distance.*

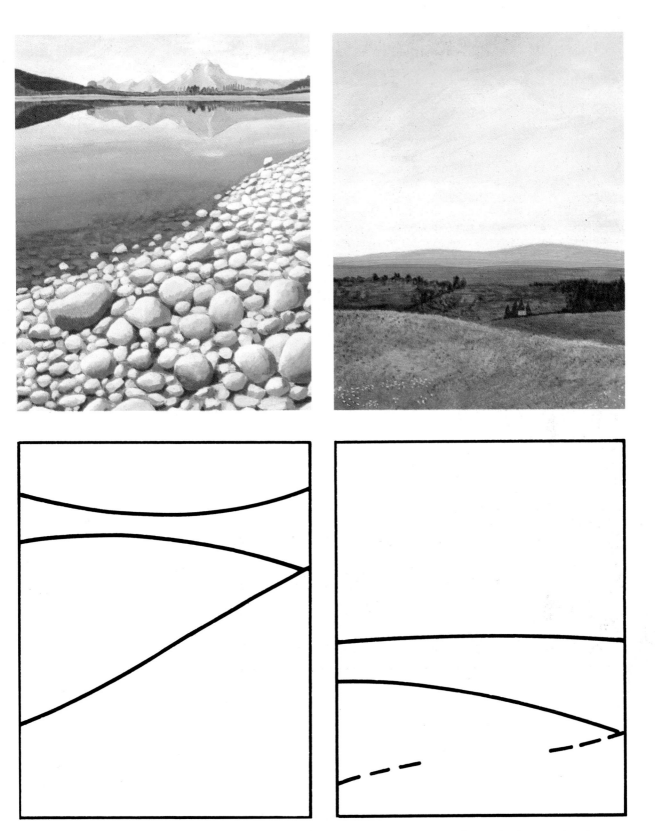

to look. To create controlled movement is not a difficult task if you consider the lines that you use and their direction; the eye will tend always to follow the length of a line – two lines in the same direction or a thick line will reinforce this tendency. The eye should, however, arrive at points which create the feeling that something similar has been seen before in the picture; this can be a device as simple as a repeated curve but it will set up a rhythm which produces unity in the whole. Good composition is a result of careful orchestration of shape, colour and line.

Space in landscape: planes

We are able to move in a landscape because it is three-dimensional; but a painted surface is flat, having only two dimensions; height and width. The problems that this raises for the painter can be resolved by use of traditional pictorial devices: linear perspective, colour perspective, and the conventions which may be derived from them.

The superimposition of various planes is one effective way of creating an illusion of depth. If you divide the distance from your position to the horizon line into three parts, you will have three separate areas to deal with.

The foreground is that plane nearest to you, the second is the middleground, and the third the background. Establish these planes immediately you begin, so that as you progress you can take each one to a different degree of finish. The background can be left lightly painted with a little more detail in the middleground. The foreground is painted with the greatest detail, thickest paint, and brightest colours, to pull it forward while the other two planes are pushed back.

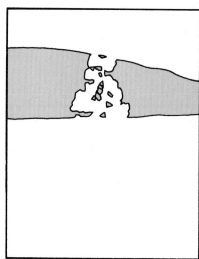

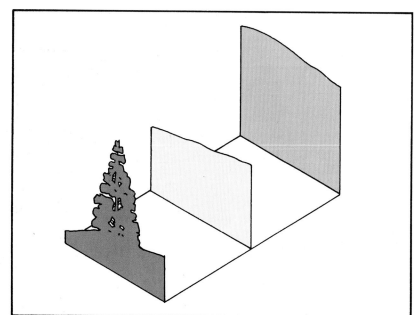

Above: *The illusion of depth can be created by treating the various areas of a scene as planes. Tonal value is the most important consideration in this kind of work.*

Left: *The planarian structure of a painting suggests space in much the same way as stage scenery.*

Opposite: *The areas of the painting at the top of the page are illustrated by the keyline diagram underneath. Notice how each plane is suggested by a difference in both strength of colour and the hardness of its edge.*

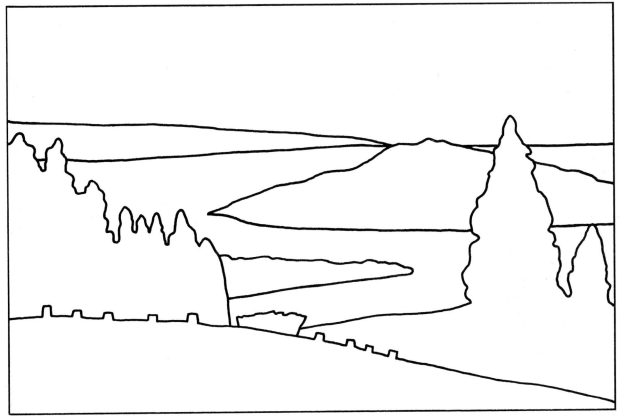

Space in landscape: linear perspective

A vast knowledge of perspective is not absolutely necessary for a landscape painter; he can achieve spatial depth convincingly by other means. There might be occasions when perspective is needed, however, and a grasp of the basic principles will be useful.

Linear perspective is a convention which was devised by architects of the fifteenth century to show their clients how their buildings would look before they were built. It should be realized that, like constructing planes on the canvas to create an illusion of depth, perspective is a convention, a tool which can be used to aid drawing from observation. There is, however, no substitute for clear observation, whatever you are drawing or painting.

The first thing to decide when doing a perspective drawing is the position of the eye level or

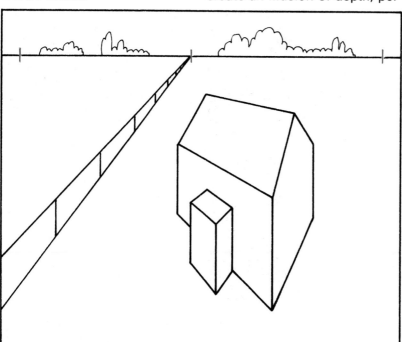

Left: *In this diagram, the eye level of the observer is high above the ground as if looking down upon the scene from the side of a hill. The fence which enters the field of vision at the lower left, meets the vanishing point on the horizon. In order to construct the house, two vanishing points are used. The basic rule of perspective is that all parallel lines meet at the same vanishing point which is always on the horizon.*

Right: *The scene viewed from a lower eye level. The same rules still apply. The vanishing points remain in the same position on the horizon line though some of the lines of the house are now angled downward because they are above eye level.*

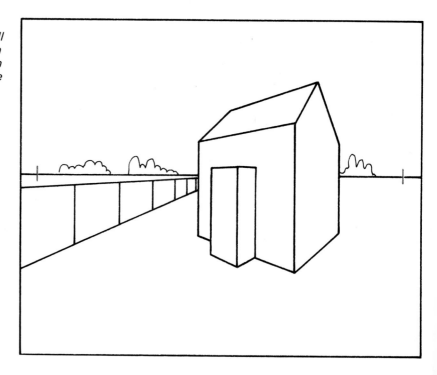

horizon line on the paper. This will depend on your position. Is it high or low?

If your eye level is high, so will be your horizon line on the paper and everything below it will slope up toward it.

If low, everything above the horizon line will slope downward to it.

If your eye level is midway, both upward and downward angles will appear equally distributed.

These angles which slope downward and upward are the core of perspective and can be seen clearly in places where the angles are most acute, such as in towns and villlages. In the open landscape, however, they are not so strongly in evidence. Use whatever clues you may find: buildings, roads, or fences.

You will observe that regular features, like a line of poles or a fence that recedes from you or even a road, will possess angles that you can assess. These angles which will slope upward toward your eye level, or downward if they are above your eye level, can be measured by holding a pencil vertically so that the angle can be assessed in relation to it.

Below: *As this drawing shows, the vanishing points will not always be contained within the confines of the picture area. The same rules of construction apply, however, and if necessary a larger sheet of backing paper could be used to check the position of the vanishing points as the work proceeds.*

Space in landscape: tonal perspective

It might not be immediately apparent, but tone plays as important a role in landscape painting as colour. A painting, to be effective, is dependent on both.

What, then, is meant by tone? Tone is the degree of lightness or darkness of a colour. As in music, if the tones are properly related the result will appear more harmonious and so be more expressive. If the tones are misjudged the result will be confused, and unattractive.

Normally, if the light is poor we cannot see colour and cannot perceive distance as efficiently. This is why, when driving a car at dusk, we find it more difficult to judge speed and distance properly. There is not sufficient light to operate those cells in our eyes which perceive colour, yet the cells still try and tend to confuse the message which reaches the brain from the cells which perceive only black and white. From a practical point of view, the eyes respond to tone more readily than they do to colour; colour is secondary.

A study of the tones of a landscape will enable you to use colour to express distance far better. If tones are graded into their proper relationship, in our drawings and paintings, the eye will accept the illusion of distance.

Grading tone is not difficult. The darkest tones are closest while the lightest appear further away. The things closest to us are stronger in tone and colour, are clearer in detail and, as they move from us in the distance they become blurred. If you make a point of emphasizing this in your paintings, you will have no difficulty in creating the illusion of great depth. Tonal colour behaves in much the same way. It is stronger in the foreground. The further away objects are, the bluer and greyer they become.

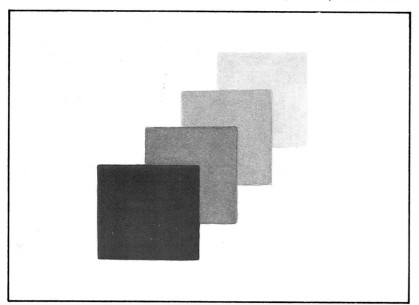

Left: *When colour is used, the illusion of depth or distance is created by employing a paler tint of the colour. However, when different colours are used each colour must be assessed tonally and this can be a little more difficult as some colours are naturally stronger than others.*

Below left: *The same diagram, this time rendered in pencil. Practise with a variety of grades of pencil until you are able to apply a constant tone to the paper both on a small and a large area.*

Above: *Selecting the correct pencil and using the correct pressure on each area is the secret of a good tonal pencil drawing. The more you practise pencil technique the more variation you will obtain as your control of the medium improves.*

Above: *When pen and ink are used, pressure is of secondary importance. The density of the mark remains the same at all times. Tonal gradation is a question of the thickness of the line and the number of lines applied to the area.*

Above: *This is a good method of learning to use paint because the problems involved are reduced. The tonal value of different colours can be ignored while you concentrate on making the painting work using white and other colour.*

Above: *When executing a full-colour painting, you will need to understand how to mix different colours to the same tonal value so that you can make areas of the painting recede or come forward as required. Practice is the key to a successful technique.*

Light, atmosphere, and contrast

Light is the most influential element for a painter. Without it nothing exists visually, so we need to pay a great deal of attention to its behaviour. It reveals not only the solidity of objects, but also the space they inhabit, and is instrumental in conveying atmosphere, mood, and the nature of colour.

The result of light falling on an object is a cast shadow. You cannot have one without the other and the depth or darkness of the shadow is related to the intensity of light. It is important to ascertain the direction from which the light comes. In landscape painting it will depend on the position of the sun, which may be high or low, to the left, right, or behind you. It may be obscured by cloud. You must take notice of these variables before you begin. Study the differences between the effects that sunlight has on the planes as they recede from you, and what kinds of shadows are thrown.

If the light is strong, the shadows will be intense. If diffused by cloud, the shadows will be softer and less obvious.

Sunlight is not constant and its quality varies throughout the day. From dawn to dusk, each period of time has its own particular mood. Similarly, changes of weather and different cloud formations will give the light, and so the mood, a different aspect. These changes will often reveal space and distance more clearly, but being transitory may have to be overemphasized to do them justice.

Light in spring and summer will tend to be warmer in colour and the shadows more crisply defined and full of contrast. In winter, the light is less intense, complicating the forms of the landscape. These different kinds of light will affect the mood and can also be exploited to create depth and a means of enhancing the composition.

Left: *The diagrams illustrate the importance of light and shadow. The top diagram appears flat and devoid of interest because the direction of the light source has been ignored. The lower two diagrams differ in both direction and colour of cast shadow, suggesting different times of the day and their attendant moods.*

Above: Farms Near Auvers by Vincent van Gogh. The painting was executed in bright colour with no reference to shadow. The result is a painting which exudes sunshine from its tapestry of brushmarks. Compare this with the painting by Norbert Goeneutte below, with its foreboding sky promising yet more snow. An unusual factor in this painting is the light colour of the ground against which all other elements stand out in sharp contrast. Note also the comparative smoothness of the paint on the canvas.

Elements of landscape: buildings

The problem involved in rendering any element of a landscape is primarily one of visualization. This means deciding exactly what you see and, subsequently, deciding how to go about painting or drawing it. Probably the most formidable task facing the newcomer to painting is the decision about what is "seen". This is because everybody knows what houses, trees, and grass look like and this knowledge impairs observation.

Our understanding of the world is built upon experience, and this means that we recognize objects by their similarity to an idea of that object carried in the mind: we have a concept of the world against which to match objects. Once this match has been made, the object has been defined and it becomes ignored for the purposes of our normal day-to-day lives. This allows our conscious mind to concentrate on the job in hand while the subconscious takes care of perception.

Learning to see

The problem facing the newcomer is formidable because, in order to be able to paint, the tendency to ignore, and the preconceived ideas allied to it, must be overcome. The people who say that they cannot paint are really saying that they cannot see and analyze their

Above and right: *The subjects on this page are treated from three different distances. Compare the amount of detail in each rendering; it is what is seen that should be included in a painting not what is known to be there. Once you have mastered your materials, observation is the key to successful work.*

vision in sufficient depth to be able to put it down on paper.

The illustrations on this and the following pages will attempt to provide some indication of the way in which a subject might be rendered, and the method of approaching the task. The activity is entirely personal, and the aim should be to find a method of working which is easiest for you. This will not be as difficult as it sounds because in art, as in all things, one person will find one method easier while another will assume a different approach which he will tend to use and develop because, for him, it is the easiest and most efficient.

Method and style

Do not be discouraged if you find that you cannot work in a particular way, or are unable to obtain a degree of finish as polished as some originals. A great part of what is known as an artist's style is simply the result of that person finding a method of working which is his own, and therefore easy for him to use, and developing it by constant practice with all kinds of materials.

There can be no hard and fast rules laid down about the way you learn to draw and paint. It will always be dependent on the stage you have reached in your development. In the early days, if you find one material easier to use, then by all means use it to the exclusion of all others until you have built up your confidence. You will often find that, later, other materials can be employed using a modified technique derived from your normal method of working.

Above and left: *The illustrations here will give you an idea of how to approach this kind of subject using watercolour. The washes are darkened gradually working from the general to the specific.*

Elements of landscape: trees

It is the elements which you include or leave out of your drawings and paintings which make the finished work look convincing. To show the character of a tree or shrub you have to know something about its structure.

Like the human body with its bones and muscles, a tree or shrub has its trunk and branches. With the human body,

however, the internal structure is permanently hidden and only seen on the dissecting table. Trees and shrubs, on the other hand, if they are deciduous, shed their covering of leaves annually.

To understand the structure of a tree or shrub means that you must study it in its dressed and undressed states; both have their part to play in describing

the form. In winter, trees without leaves have just as much dignity and beauty as when fully laden.

Structure

A tree or shrub is made up of many small shapes. Apart from the main trunk, the branches, twigs, and shoots are a mass of elongated forms. The leaves which clothe the tree are further

Above and left: *Analyze the form and structure of trees in your landscape first. If the early definition is lightly drawn subsequent drawing or painting can be carried out without the need to erase the initial statement.*

Above: *Notice the difference in the treatment of foliage when it is further away. Attempting to paint every leaf individually would have resulted in a lifeless and unnatural appearance.*

numerous small shapes. If you attempt to draw a tree or shrub by concentrating on these small shapes the result will look unconvincing.

You should aim to work broadly and construct the overall shape of the tree, breaking the larger shapes into smaller ones as you proceed in order to avoid making a tight and laboured image. Always work from the general toward the specific.

The character of trees and shrubs changes when seen in groups. Singly they may look static, but in a mass they take on rhythms and movements created by variations of colour and shape. The colour of trees and shrubs when contrasted with each other may also appear quite different than when seen singly.

Because of their structure, trees also possess a textural quality and pattern, which may change under certain circumstances; in the wind, in a raking, strong side light, or when contrasted with smooth, even backgrounds each tree will project a different character.

This textural quality or pattern will vary appreciably with the type of leaf. Some are thick and luscious, others thin and wispy; while painting, grasp it early, and depict it loosely and with feeling for the form.

It is worth keeping a sketchbook in which to practise drawing and painting trees, both in detail and from a distance.

Above and left: *A step-by-step illustration of the method of painting a tree at a distance and the treatment of a tree trunk when seen at close quarters.*

Elements of landscape: skies and clouds

The sky is vastly important in landscape painting. Its tone, colour, and light affects every part of the terrain. It can take up two-thirds of a canvas and be the prime subject or be reduced to a tiny strip at the top. Even so, the ground will reflect the character of the sky.

Skies vary with time of day. They may be intense in colour or subtly tinted, depending on whether it is dawn, dusk, or midday. They may be clear or cloudy. If related to a strongly toned foreground, the sky will appear pale, conversely, if there is a great deal of sunlight on the ground, the sky will be rich and dense in colour.

The appearance of a sky is rarely static. It is the inconstancy of sky and the light which comes from it which causes the rapid and radical change in the appearance of all the other elements in a landscape.

A sky is not like a curtain with the same hue from top to bottom. The gradations that take place are from dark above to lighter toward the horizon. If the sky is a rich blue overhead, it will become a lighter blue as it meets the horizon. The changes of colour need not necessarily be of the same hue. Blue may turn to green or purple, and at dusk or dawn the sky may be shot with red, orange, and yellow. The colours may move through the whole spectrum; that is the source of its fascination. Learn to detect these changes, and use your brush either vigorously or smoothly to express the variations of depth and tone to enhance the particular qualities of skies at different times.

Nothing can change a sky more swiftly than clouds, which may either be blown across or appear to form before your very eyes.

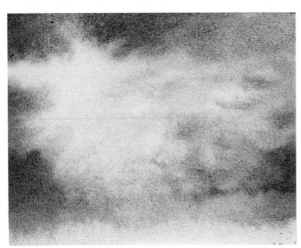

Above left: *The technique used will vary with different skies. Here, watercolour was laid onto damp paper to create an effect of sunlight breaking through clouds after rain.*

Above right: *The contrast of an evening sky is best rendered by allowing each wash to dry to create a hard edge to the clouds.*

Right: *A combination of both techniques will often be necessary.*

Cloud formations alter so considerably, and so quickly that only by constant observation can you learn to record their individual characteristics. As Constable did, keep a record of them in a notebook devoted solely to the way clouds behave. It will be useful for the production of compositions later, as well as improving your knowledge of the types of cloud and ways of painting them.

Bear in mind that, although clouds are basically gaseous and weightless, they do reflect light, and often appear quite shapely and solid. Like solid forms, they possess clearly defined light and dark areas.

Clouds are literally suspended in space. To give the impression of depth, treat them as you would objects on the ground by the use of perspective and scale.

Cloud formations affect the landscape by creating rhythms and movements which echo or contrast with the forms beneath.

Top: *Two stages in the production of a skyscape using the alla prima method of oil painting. The first colours should be thinly applied to facilitate the laying in of the whites without destroying the colours.*

Above and below: *Three stages in the production of a sky using the traditional method of oil painting. Paint thinned with oil (known as a glaze) is painted over previously applied areas to intensify the effect.*

Elements of landscape: water

The qualities and character of large expanses of water such as seas, rivers, and lakes are quite different to small confined areas of water as in ponds, streams, and puddles. Most of the differences are due to the way light falls on the surface of the water because of the existence or lack of surrounding forms and how much movement there is.

The ripple of water is generally caused by wind or current. Sometimes, however, it is caused by birds, fish, boats, and people. Whatever the cause, water will reflect what is around and above it. The larger the area of water, the more of the sky it will reflect. Small areas of contained water are more likely to be still, and so will reflect with the clarity of a mirror.

Areas of water rarely look the same because winds and currents are not constant. The flowing stream one day may look like plate glass the next; you can never be sure how the surface will appear. The sky will also play its part and affect the reflection, so study all of them, static as well as fast-moving water, ripples as well as waves.

The following points should be borne in mind: though water always reflects what is around and above, the colour reflected is always lower in tone than the original. Movement will fragment the reflection, slight movements interrupting the reflection without making it unrecognizable, strong movement completely obliterating it.

Left: *The changeable nature of water is reflected in these sketchbook extracts. The character changes according to the elements acting upon it and this is probably the fascination of water.*

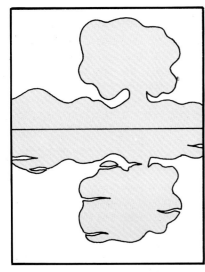

Above: *Note how, when all else remains the same, the break-up of the reflection in the water suggests varying degrees of movement.*

Left: *Refraction causes a great deal of difference also. Compare these two views of the same object. Note how the colour value of the subject has changed.*

Below: *Monet began making studies of this lily pond during his mature period. The constantly changing character of its surface and depths held an allure which captivated him for the rest of his life.*

Methods of drawing: observation

When beginning to draw, experimentation with different materials is important, as is analysis of the structures of trees, rocks, and clouds. Draw freely and often and do not be put off by apparent failure. Keep all your drawings, even the bad ones. You may be surprised later looking back at them and they can provide a record of how much you have improved as you practise.

Making a start

To be confronted with a blank sheet of paper, a pencil, and a magnificent panorama can be as daunting for the experienced as for the beginner. How do you start? At what point can you decide that you have captured the essence of the scene?

The first thing to remember is not to try too hard. When you first look at a landscape, your immediate reaction will be complex. It will be difficult to unravel your feelings right away so do not try. Sit down and have a good long stare letting your eyes rove over the scene to let the overall image soak in. Do not make any effort to analyze what

you see, but accept it uncritically. Absorb it like a sponge. Make a few, simple, lightly drawn marks on your paper, indicating those aspects of the landscape which you find important. Making heavy, dark marks on white paper too soon only adds to the difficulties you are trying to resolve. Draw with light, broken lines or dots to get the "feel" of the pencil on the paper.

These marks are only exploratory and there is no need to erase them should they appear to be in the wrong place. Leave them as a guide, against which to gauge corrections.

Add a few scribbles of tone. Scribbled or smudged tones, drawn gently, will also help you get the "feel" of the pencil on the paper. The tones will advance the drawing and make the image more convincing.

To bring what you are drawing into sharper focus, look more at the scene in front of you and less at your drawing. Paradoxically, looking more at your drawing and less at the scene is likely to confuse the image rather than clarify it. Concentrating on the scene allows your hand to respond instinctively and so carry out its job more naturally.

Trust the process of looking and letting the pencil make marks without effort, and curb your desire to criticize and interfere with what emerges on the paper. By being too critical you destroy the natural flow, fail to enjoy what you are doing, and cause the drawing to become contrived.

Allow your drawing to become gradually darker and stronger in tone until all the paper is covered. This will give you confidence. By pushing your drawings too far initially, you will learn how far you need to go.

Drawing outdoors using this method can be done in a sketchbook or on paper clipped to a light drawing board and held on your knee. An easel is not as necessary as it would be for oil painting but do hold your board or sketchbook upright from time to time to compare what you are doing with what you are looking at. Stand away from your drawing, and view it from a distance by placing it upright against a wall or stone, or even on the ground. "Distancing" yourself from your work allows you to respond to it more objectively.

Left: *During the early stages of a drawing, it can be helpful to use a pencil held at arm's length to measure the relative proportions of elements in the landscape. However, use it only as an initial guide or your drawing may become cramped and stiff.*

Above right: *The first lines of a drawing lightly laid in.*

Centre right: *Reinforcement of the initial statement with some tone added.*

Below right: *The completed drawing. Note the slight emphasis placed upon the pier; compare this with the photograph of the scene on the opposite page.*

Methods of drawing: selection

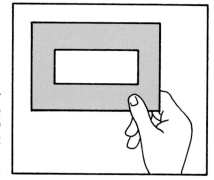

The first step in drawing landscapes is to spend time looking before making exploratory marks in line and tone. The second step is to be more selective in what you choose and the way it is interpreted through emphasis.

Emphasizing the important aspects of what you see will make your work more effective, and so more pleasing to look at. But they must be aspects which you find important; do not be led, for subconsciously you know what is important to you.

As has been pointed out, nature is not confined to a rectangle. Neither are your eyes restricted to the accepted range of 60 degrees. By moving your head or letting your eyes rove over a scene, you can take in 180 degrees at a glance without moving your body.

You can either try to draw the whole panorama or select a particular area that appeals to you, not only across the landscape, but into it as well.

If you use your eyes like the lens of a camera that can zoom in on a part and enlarge it, to the exclusion of what borders it, you will find that you can filter out what you do not need of a distant scene and enlarge the section you want. If it is too close, then you can reduce it.

To show how this works, try looking at a scene through a rectangle cut out of a piece of card, preferably black. By holding the card nearer or further away from you, you can completely alter the view you are looking at. If you move the card across the scene you will be amazed how different the views are when isolated in this way by the card viewfinder. As you gain experience, you will find you can dispense with the viewfinder.

Emphasis

When you select a part from the whole, your choice places an emphasis on that part as being special. It is quite possible to select a number of parts for emphasis yet find the view as a whole uninteresting or unmanageable. On the other hand, you might find that the whole view and its parts deserve attention.

Opposite: *A viewfinder can be cut from a piece of card.*

Right and below: *Two drawings produced from the viewpoint shown opposite. Almost anything can provide a subject for a good drawing: that is the fascination of landscape work.*

Methods of oil painting: alla prima

There are as many ways to paint in oils as there are painters, each has his own method of expression. But fundamental to any personally evolved method are two basic styles which underlie all others: the direct method or Alla Prima, and the Traditional method.

Completing a painting in one session in full colour, with opaque paint so that any previous drawing or underpainting tends to be obliterated and has little or no modifying effect on the subsequent layers, is referred to as "Alla Prima." It was first used in the nineteenth century when many painters began painting landscapes directly in the open air.

It is a method that landscape painters still favour today because it is an ideal way of completing a painting when there are problems with the weather or available time. It may also better suit your temperament.

Affinities with the Traditional method do exist so that you do not need to turn somersaults to accommodate both styles. Learning about one will help the other. For example, you can draw in your composition as you would with the Traditional method, or make preparatory studies or sketches beforehand. It is, however, essentially painting in one go and preparation is not necessary except for the underpainting or priming coat of paint.

Tonal priming

The essential point about oil painting is that, since it is an opaque or obliterating medium, you can organize your tones more convincingly if you start from the middle to dark end of the tonal scale rather than from the lightest: the white canvas.

Very simply this means that, unlike watercolour where you work from light to dark for the best results, with oil you work more from dark to light. However, for practical purposes it is best to start with the mid range of tones so that you can gauge more accurately the intensity of the lights and darks.

To facilitate this part of the process, ensure that your surfaces have a light to medium tone on them before you begin. Prior to going out, prepare a thin

Left: *The scene from which the painting on these pages was produced. Note how closely the colours of the original subject have been followed.*

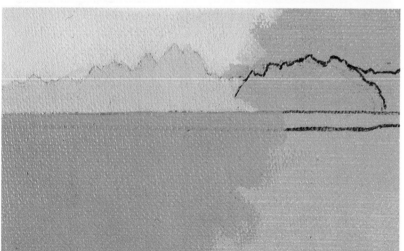

Left: *The initial stages of the painting. The left-hand side of the painting has the first flat colours laid in while the right-hand side shows the tonal priming of the canvas and the basic drawing.*

creamy mixture of a quick-drying foundation white (some artist's colourmen make a specially prepared white for this purpose). This is tinted with a little raw umber and your support is covered completely with it. It does not matter if the result is streaky as this will help animate your painting. Do make sure that there are no ridges of thick paint in evidence as this will interfere with your one-coat Alla Prima effect.

Drying mediums

The problem with Alla Prima painting is that, if your paint is too wet, the effects you require may not be easy to produce. Additionally, if your painting is wet, when completed these effects may be spoiled. It is worth experimenting with a drying medium which will resolve the problem without interfering with the way you paint.

Above right: The foreground, background, and sky have been worked up to their correct tonal balance.

Centre right: The line of the trees has been broadly applied; the paler trees will be painted over and into these to push them back.

Below right: The completed painting. The foreground is laid in with just enough detail to prevent it detracting from the centre of interest – the trees and mountain range behind. In a composition of this nature it is the abstract quality of the bands of colour and texture which are important.

There are many kinds available but the most successful is the newest type made with an alkyd resin which is safe and easy to use. It will not damage the painted surface by cracking as it dries and is pleasant to paint with. You can use it in your dipper, either neat or diluted with turpentine, depending on how quickly you want the paint to dry. There are also two thicker versions which will help to create an effective impasto.

Methods of oil painting: traditional

The Traditional method of painting is slower than Alla Prima because there are more stages involved in the process. It is the ideal method if you want a more considered approach which will produce a greater degree of finish in the completed work.

The Traditional method can be used outdoors or in the studio. Working inside will be considered in the next section but, whichever you do, an easel is an essential piece of equipment. It will allow you the freedom to concentrate on mixing colours properly and to see clearly what you are doing and how you are progressing. By standing back from the easel, you can relate more easily what you are looking at in the landscape with how you are painting it. Moreover, it is easier to paint on a vertical support and it cuts out unwanted reflected light that might make the painted surface shine unpleasantly while you are working.

To begin, define precisely the part of the landscape you are going to paint as you may have to work from it for more than one session. Make a number of preliminary studies of your subject first, in the manner suggested in the section on drawing.

Prepare your surfaces before going out, with a mid-toned tint of raw umber and white.

When you are satisfied with your viewpoint, draw the basic composition on the tinted surface with charcoal pencil or a brush and diluted raw umber paint. Keep it simple, almost diagrammatic, avoiding detail.

When the drawing is dry, commence painting over it with colour. This too should be broad but near in colour and tone to what you are looking at.

Above: *A painting completed using the Traditional method of oil painting. The main difference between Alla Prima and traditional methods of painting is the thickness of the paint used for the overpainting. When painting a subject in one go, the paint does not have sufficient time to dry. Therefore, to prevent unwanted mixing of the colours, the paint is applied more thickly. The traditional approach, on the other hand, allows the paint a certain amount of drying time and subsequent coats are often applied more thinly so that the underpainting glows through creating greater depth and more subtle, jewel-like qualities. For example, when a green is required it is quite possible to underpaint using yellow and follow this with a thin glaze of blue. The result will glow with an inner life and intensity that is lacking in a single coat of opaque colour. It remains possible, as with the Alla Prima method of painting, to correct mistakes by scraping out and repainting the area with new colour. The area cleaned should be reasonably dry before the new coat of paint is applied to the surface. When scraping paint from the canvas it can be difficult to remove every scrap of pigment because of the grain. Don't be over fussy about this, as long as they are dry, small remnants can be left to modify the surface adding texture and interest to the area.*

As you will be working on the painting for some time, spend plenty of time simply looking and mixing and proportionally less in painting. Painting too rapidly can lead to muddled and muddy colours in the end result.

The process can be summed up as: broad shapes first, moving gradually to smaller and more precise shapes. Detail last, freely executed brush strokes first, more carefully controlled brush marks last, thin paint first, fat or thick paint later.

Changing your mind as often as the situation demands is eminently possible with oils if you observe these conditions, and doing so is a necessary part of producing a good painting.

Right: *The painting in its first stage. The basic drawing has been done and the areas filled in with flat colour.*

Right: *Some basic background detail has been added and the clouds have been blocked in.*

Right: *The clouds and mountains are more fully modelled and the painting requires only the foreground detail to complete it.*

Studies for an oil painting

Working in the studio, rather than outdoors, allows more freedom to use memory and imagination but, as the only reference to landscape will be through your notes and studies, it will involve a slightly different approach to be certain they are used to advantage.

Working indoors may be forced upon you by bad weather, or other circumstances beyond your control. To take some previously made drawings and watercolours and work them up into an oil painting is as good a way of expressing yourself as being in front of the real thing.

Above: *This study was produced from the scene shown in the photograph on the left. Remembering that you can never have too much information from which to work, as much detail as possible was worked into the drawing.*

Firstly, it will be appreciated that working on the spot will furnish valuable experience that will aid memory, but if you intend to rely on drawings and colour sketches which are too brief or too few, they will fail either to jog the memory or stimulate the imagination. Therefore both experience and thorough studies should be your aim when working outside.

Drawings for this process should be concerned with detail as well as broad statements, light and atmosphere, changes of weather, formations of clouds, studies of trees, both in the form of drawings and coloured and written notes.

As a result studies may only be fragments of information, but as long as they are carefully observed they will be of value.

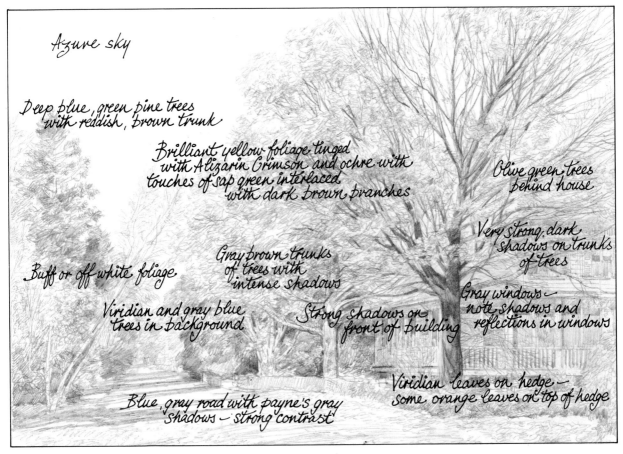

Azure sky

Deep blue, green pine trees with reddish, brown trunk

Brilliant yellow foliage tinged with Alizarin Crimson and ochre with touches of sap green interlaced with dark brown branches

Olive green trees behind house

Very strong, dark shadows on trunks of trees

Buff or off white foliage

Gray brown trunks of trees with intense shadows

Gray windows – note shadows and reflections in windows

Viridian and gray blue trees in background

Strong shadows on front of building

Blue, gray road with payne's gray shadows – strong contrast

Viridian leaves on hedge – some orange leaves on top of hedge

Above: *An alternative method of making colour notes is to write them on a sheet of tracing paper fixed to the original study.*

Left: *Detail abstracted from the foreground of the scene for special attention. It is worth studying man-made structures in the landscape as these are the things that can be difficult to work from memory.*

Completing an oil painting

Completing an oil painting in the studio from sketches and studies relies, in the initial stages, on composition. It helps you select the best possible subject by choosing views that accord best with the format you are using and deploying the shapes and colours to the best possible effect by paying attention to the dynamics of the forms you are observing.

Composition is used in the studio in much the same way except that you have the flexibility to select and arrange the raw material – sketches and studies – in any way you wish. You are not restricted by what is in front of you as you would be outside. You can distribute the colours and forms in the way that you feel is appropriate. Your choices will still be limited by the shape and, possibly, the size of your support, and the way you assemble your material will have to take into consideration the basic principles discussed in the section on composition.

Having said this, you will discover as you work that you can make as many alternative arrangements as you like until you are satisfied everything is presented in the best possible way for the purpose intended.

Making a number of exploratory rough drawings from your initial sketches is a practical way of ensuring that the "happiest" solution is arrived at. You can then enlarge the best of them to the size you wish to use for the painting and transfer the drawing to your painting surface. You can begin drawing straight onto the support or scale it up first by squaring.

Once you have transferred your composition to the tinted surface, the procedure for carrying out the painting is much the same as suggested in the previous section. The only difference is that you must rely on memory and imagination to replace an actual landscape in front of you. Substitute your memory and imagination for the landscape and use your drawings and studies as props. The drawing need not be strictly adhered to should you find that your creative impulses are fighting to be unleashed.

Painting indoors away from any kind of landscape that you can refer to is perhaps the most enjoyable way to express yourself. On the other hand, it is more difficult for the inexperienced. If you persevere, however, and practise both kinds of approach, you will find that each will help the other to progress.

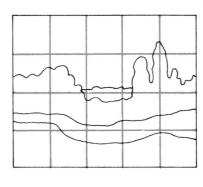

A canvas of similar proportion is selected to receive the enlarged drawing and both surfaces are squared as shown here.

Right: *The process of squaring up a drawing is quite a simple one. The number of squares used is not important as long as there are enough to provide sufficient guidance. It should also be remembered, that the proportions of the two surfaces must be the same.*

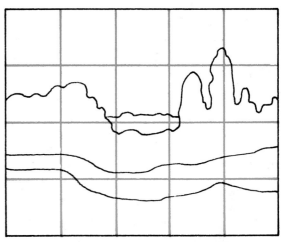

Below: *The painting completed in the studio following the sequence of steps shown on the opposite page. The initial drawing was produced from the studies on the previous page with alteration made to improve the composition.*

Foregrounds

Foregrounds play such an important role in landscape painting that they are well worth studying separately. Landscape painters, both past and present, have relied a great deal on what could be done with a foreground and their work will repay study.

When looking at a landscape that you may want to paint, it is quite easy to overlook the foreground. The tendency is to look for the middle and background, quite forgetting that the scene before you starts at your feet.

The great landscape painters were always careful to examine the foreground in case they missed something valuable.

Many painters, for instance, pay so much attention to the foreground that it takes up most of the painting and becomes the subject and focal point. Derelict barns, walls, fences, hedges, pools, ponds, gates, farm machinery, fallen trees, waterfalls, in short, anything that takes your eye can serve as a subject, or a good foreground.

Generally, foregrounds are included to give the landscape more life, or more authenticity. A foreground well-established in the composition will give balance to whatever else is included. It can also help to suggest space. It can lead the eye into the picture to where you want your visual emphasis. It can be used to fill parts of the

painting that would otherwise be devoid of interest.

There is no end to the versatility of the foreground, provided that you pay attention to it when you are out sketching. Once you are familiar with the visual characteristics: large, clear, strongly coloured, the foreground will assert itself more firmly in your paintings.

Make a point from time to time of studying foregrounds only. Fill a notebook with different kinds. You will never regret doing so as these drawings will always be useful when you are working in the studio. If it does nothing else, the experience will make you more conscious of their contribution and will increase your observational skills.

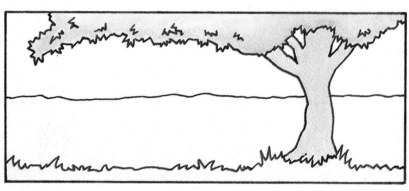

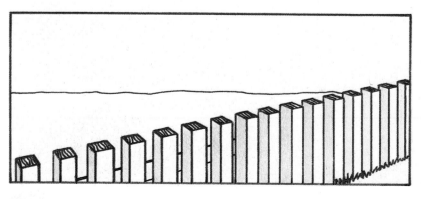

Top left: *The tree and grass in the foreground is used as a device to frame the middle and background.*

Centre left: *In this illustration the foreground motif is the focal point and is supported by the background.*

Below left: *The foreground again used as a device, this time to lead the eye across and into the picture.*

Opposite top: *Detail from* Long Grass with Butterflies *by van Gogh, a superb painting in which the foreground is the subject relying upon colour and the brush mark to provide interest.*

Opposite bottom: *In this detail from Monet's painting,* Bathers at la Grenouillere, *the boats in the foreground lead the eye to the focal point of the painting – the bathers silhouetted against the light entering under the trees.*

95

PEOPLE
Making a mark

Before setting out to tackle any specific subject, it is very important that you have a working understanding of the widely differing properties and characteristics of the various materials available. You will probably, after having gained more experience, begin to establish your own preferences, but it is worth experimenting with as many as possible to begin with.

With pencils, practise varying the pressure in shading to learn control, and even when drawing a single line, to produce "accents" in its quality. Similarly, with charcoal or chalks, practise grading tones by rubbing and smudging the strokes with thumb or a rolled piece of paper. With any of these materials, experiment with various combinations, including lightly washed-in watercolour.

Tone can also be described using pen and ink, a purely line

Key:
1. F graphite pencil
2. HB graphite pencil
3. charcoal pencil
4. willow charcoal
5. 2B graphite pencil
6. 3B graphite pencil
7. red conté crayon
8. brown conté crayon
9. 6B graphite pencil
10. Wolff's carbon pencil
11. black conté crayon
12. pastel

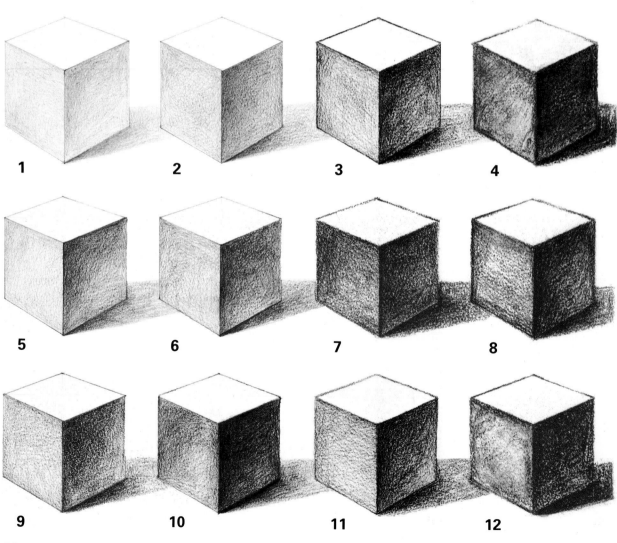

1   2   3   4

5   6   7   8

9   10   11   12

medium. This is suggested by "cross-hatching" and building up areas of delicate lines close together. A wide range of tones can be indicated by this method, especially when used in conjunction with watercolour washes. Do experiment with a variety of papers and background tints.

When using coloured pencils, try building up areas of colour by superimposing more than one colour as this will lend vitality to the finished result.

The diagrams of simple cubes on these pages show the variety and depth of tonal quality possible with the materials commonly associated with figure drawing. The F, HB, and 2B pencils, correctly sharpened, are admirable for crisp, incisive drawing. 3B to 6B are better suited to broader, quicker tonal work, while carbon pencils, charcoal, and conté produce a denser range without the unpleasant shine of lead instruments.

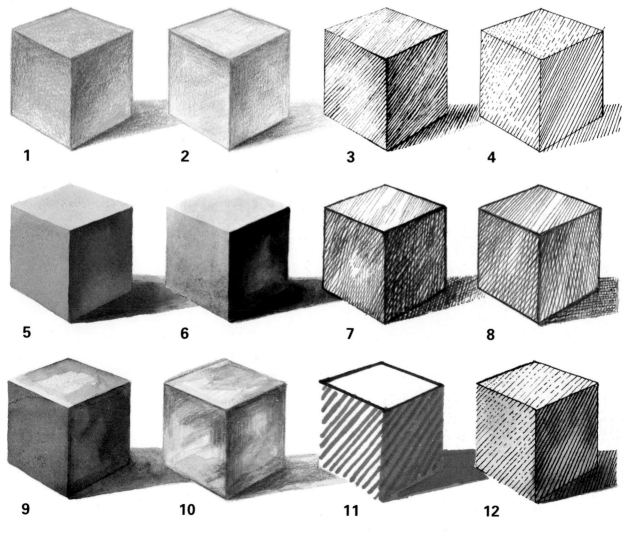

1   2   3   4

5   6   7   8

9   10   11   12

Learning to see

The act of drawing can be divided into two main areas: the intuitive and the analytical. The process of drawing involves a continual dialogue between the two, although the emphasis will depend on the type of drawing being made.

The process of perception

Light enters the eye reflected from the object and falls on the retina. The information is passed to the brain. The brain then instructs the hand to make certain marks, and evaluates those marks in relation to the subject, deciding if and how to correct them. This process is continued until the drawing is complete.

To start with, the act of drawing will be predominantly analytical, but as you gain experience and learn about colour, form, and texture, your intuitive or emotional response will show through more and more. In other words, you will acquire a visual language or vocabulary with which to guide the movements of hand and medium. The establishment of this vocabulary is absolutely essential if the artist is to bring order and clarity to his intuitive response. Without it, it is almost impossible for the artist to faithfully reflect creative attitudes to the subject he wishes to describe.

Optical illusion

Although our intuitive response to form is important for developing a feeling for the movement and angles of the figure, we need to consider consciously

Above: *The arrowheads have a misleading effect, making the line with outward-projecting arrowheads seem longer.*

the relationships between proportions and masses. Unless this is done, it is possible for our eyes to be misled, as in the diagram shown here where two lines of *equal* length appear to be unequal because of the effect of the arrowheads.

The cone of vision

The human eye has a "cone" of vision of about 60 degrees, i.e.,

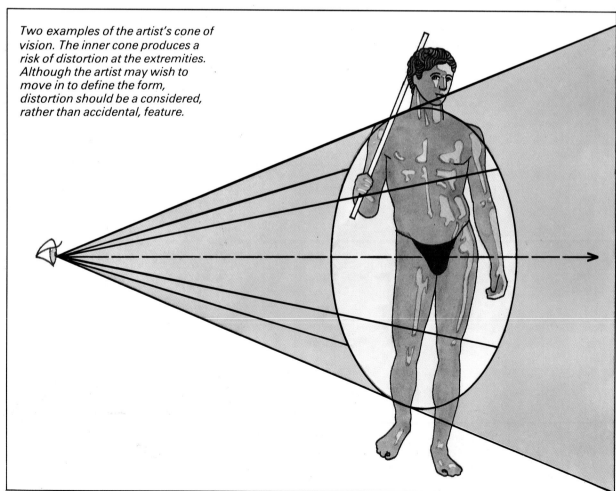

Two examples of the artist's cone of vision. The inner cone produces a risk of distortion at the extremities. Although the artist may wish to move in to define the form, distortion should be a considered, rather than accidental, feature.

about 30 degrees either side of the line of sight. Beyond this area distortions occur. Unless seeking a particular dramatic effect, it is best to position yourself no nearer than 6 feet from a seated figure and 10 feet from a standing one, in order to be able to take in the whole figure without moving your head.

To ascertain direction
A true vertical is best obtained with a plumbline and bob, or by setting up the drawing surface on the vertical plane and using the edge to give you a visual reference.

Compare any angle in the subject with an imaginary or actual vertical or horizontal before drawing it. For curves, it is useful to imagine a straight line running from one end of the curve to the other to help you assess the direction and degree of acuteness.

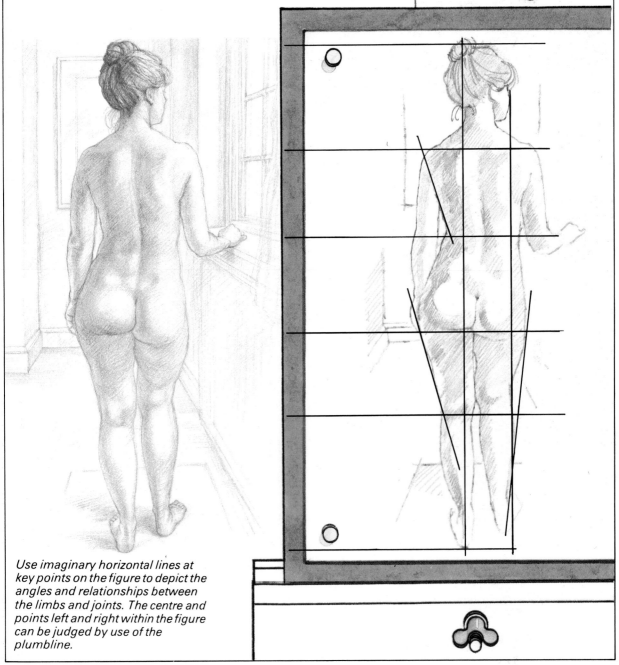

Use imaginary horizontal lines at key points on the figure to depict the angles and relationships between the limbs and joints. The centre and points left and right within the figure can be judged by use of the plumbline.

Aids to scale and proportion

Pencil measurements

Hold the pencil at arm's length toward the subject. Use the thumbnail to measure the apparent relative measurements from the pencil tip and transfer them to the paper. Provided that your arm remains straight, these measurements will all be proportionate. Never measure until you have already made a rough, intuitive sketch which can then be adjusted.

Distortion of scale

There tends to be a distortion of scale when drawing with the board resting on a "donkey" or chair, so a mental adjustment is necessary. When drawing on an easel, this will not be required as the drawing surface will be closer to eye level. If you are right-handed, look to the left of the easel so that the drawing hand and arm are not in the line of sight, and vice versa for left-handers. When using a chair or "donkey" keep the drawing board top clear of the subject.

Above: *Assessing scale by pencil measurement.*

Left: *With the board at an angle, a conscious adjustment must be made to avoid distortion. Always try to view the board at right angles.*

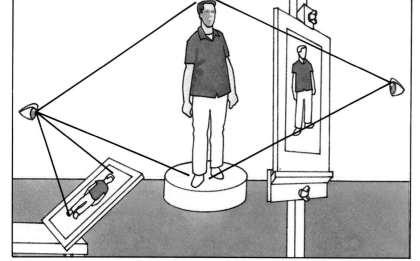

Exercises

1 – Scale and direction

Pin onto a wall or board random lengths of tape, wood strips or string up to about 4 feet long, stretched between thumbtacks. Concentrate on drawing as accurately as possible the lengths in relation to each other.

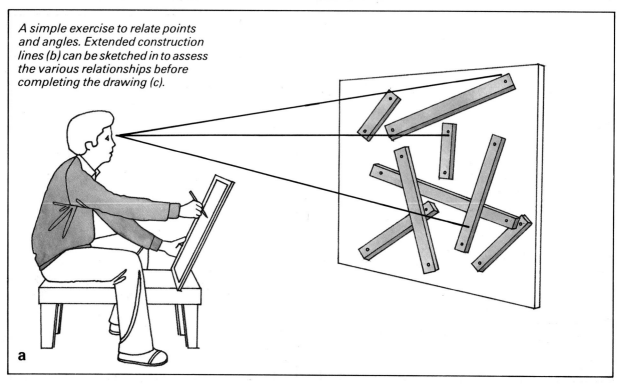

A simple exercise to relate points and angles. Extended construction lines (b) can be sketched in to assess the various relationships before completing the drawing (c).

a

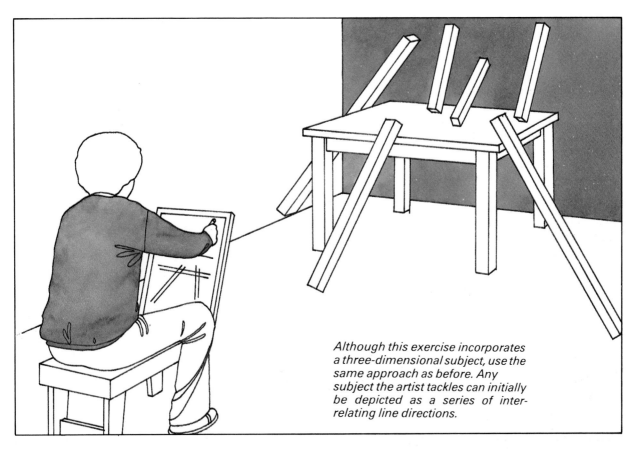

Although this exercise incorporates a three-dimensional subject, use the same approach as before. Any subject the artist tackles can initially be depicted as a series of inter-relating line directions.

2 – Proportions and angles

Place a table against a wall and arrange lengths of timber at random. Some will be sloping away from you and their proportions will be much harder to assess in a drawing. After drawing them intuitively, try to correct the drawing by using imaginary verticals and horizontals to relate the ends of each object in order to establish their positions in relation to each other (see the example illustrated on page 99.)

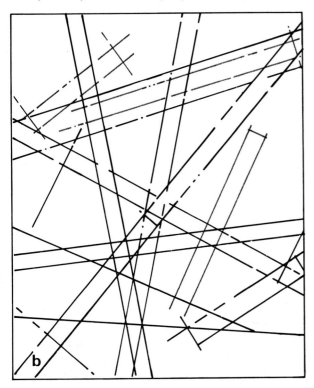

b

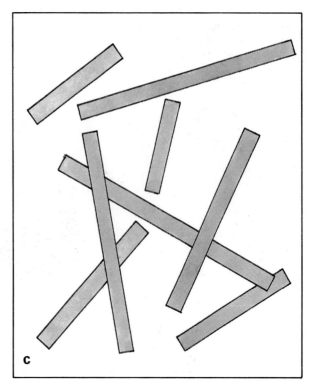

c

Perceiving form

It is an interesting fact that the mind always seeks to identify shapes as objects it knows. For example, the random line in figure 1 leaves a and b as empty areas, while the random line in figure 2 suggests the profile of a face and space d appears as a solid form.

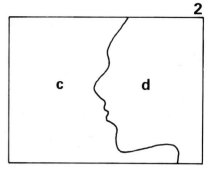

Negative shapes

When drawing the silhouette or flat shape of a figure on a blank, framed surface or picture plane, another shape is left between it and the outer edge. The figure we see as the positive shape, and the surrounding area as space. The consideration of both kinds of shape is of equal importance in drawing. In assessing the relationship between the shapes, both positive and negative should be viewed as being on the same plane and as flat areas bounded by qualities of line and tone, but without a sense of depth.

Paradoxically, the nature of the shapes seen on this "flat" plane will determine their position and scale in space. This thinking "flat," at various stages of the drawing, is essential for relating objects and figures to each other and for relating parts of the figure to the whole image. For example, if the standing figure has its hands on its hips, the space between the arm and the torso helps to relate the two parts accurately. So, too, in relating a seated figure to her chair, we must draw the shapes between the model's legs and the chair legs to correctly relate the model's legs to each other.

The third dimension

The outline/silhouette, or positive and negative shapes, are insufficient in themselves to recreate the three-dimensional aspect of the subject, as figure 3 indicates. The projection of the form can be shown as in figure 4, but even now it is difficult to decide whether we are seeing the boxes from above or below. In fact, we can read the forms

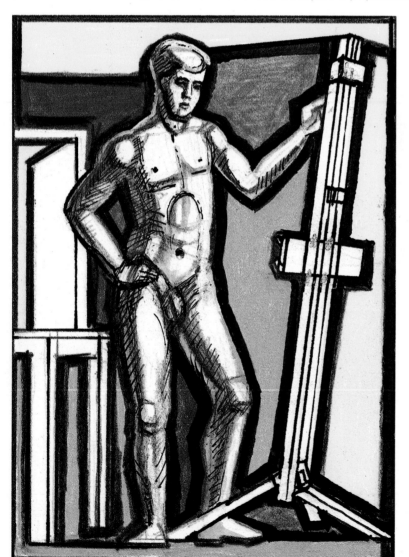

Left: *Three uses of negative shape are shown here: i) relating parts of the same object (the legs, the arms and head); ii) relating different objects such as the easel and model; iii) creating an interesting pictorial design between the main objects and the edge of the picture.*

Right: *The use of negative shape to indicate scale, as between the foreground and background figures.*

either way. By stressing the nearest planes of the boxes, using, for example, a thicker line, as in figure 5, we can decide that we are seeing them from a low eye level.

Finally, by observing two such boxes in this position more closely (figure 6), we see that the receding sides have their lines converging on an imaginary point and are not actually parallel. This is called perspective, and if observed correctly, it will remove all ambiguities.

When drawing a head and shoulders, as in figure 7, it will help to keep this solid-block construction in mind. In this diagram, the blocks are superimposed to show where the main "corners" or major changes of plane take place. Obviously, there are no hard lines or corners in the human figure, so we must work within this imaginary geometric shape, using tonal gradations or contour lines to show the real form.

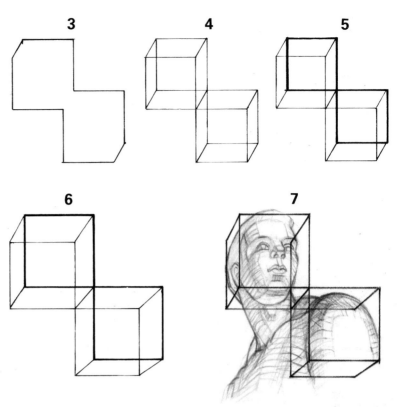

3   **4**   **5**

6   **7**

Analyzing movement

Even in a static subject like a still-life there can be as much "movement" as in a drawing of a galloping horse. True pictorial movement, as opposed to literal movement, is due to the interplay between directional lines, suggesting angles and curves between salient points. These directional lines can be either actual or implied, and this applies as much to a seated or standing figure as to one which is running or walking.

The composition created by the relationship of these main directional lines of figure and background alters as we walk around the model in search of a suitable drawing position, and should influence our eventual choice. Without a strong, exciting design, created by these lines, the figure drawing will lack vitality, however much detail is put into the finished image.

Finding a direction

Always look for the main directions of the pose, as indicated by the torso, head, and limbs, before concentrating on details. A poor composition, however accurate in execution, will not present the figure as a convincing whole.

The main directions in the figure are not necessarily the outlines, but are often imaginary lines or axial directions of the skeleton running through the middle of the outward forms. The construction lines produce the vital "push-and-pull" effect of the forms in space. They often begin and end at the joints of the skeleton.

Although these directions must be "felt" intuitively at first, we can check for accuracy later with pencil and plumbline as described earlier. Indeed, as the drawing progresses, the linking of points by extending these construction lines horizontally, vertically, and diagonally can create lines of reference on which the entire figure is to be based. For example, a line of gravity identified in a standing figure running vertically from head to ankle will help in assessing other directions.

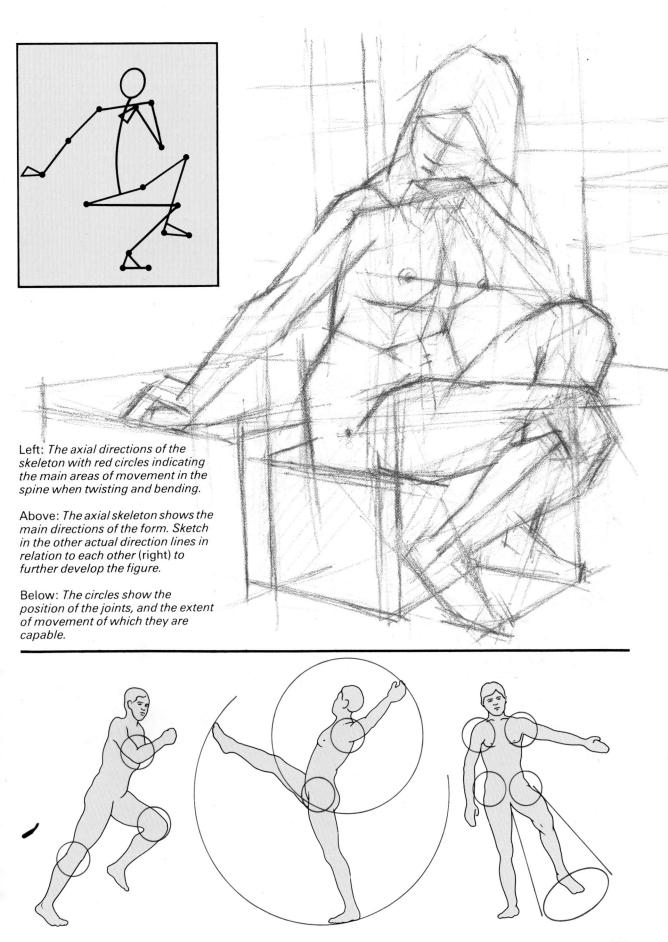

Left: *The axial directions of the skeleton with red circles indicating the main areas of movement in the spine when twisting and bending.*

Above: *The axial skeleton shows the main directions of the form. Sketch in the other actual direction lines in relation to each other* (right) *to further develop the figure.*

Below: *The circles show the position of the joints, and the extent of movement of which they are capable.*

Constructing form

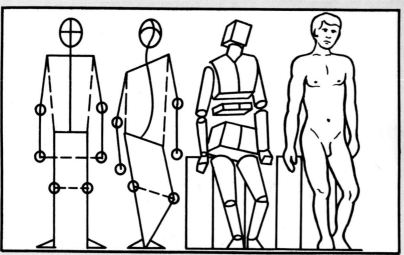

Before developing detail and subtlety of form, we must learn to think of the figure as a series of solid volumes which can move in relation to one another. The underlying forms of these volumes can be viewed as simple blocks based on the cube, cylinder, or sphere. Artists throughout history have based their initial visual consideration of a figure on this principle.

The most important blocks or masses are the upper and lower thorax (rib cage and pelvic girdle), which govern the position and direction of the blocks

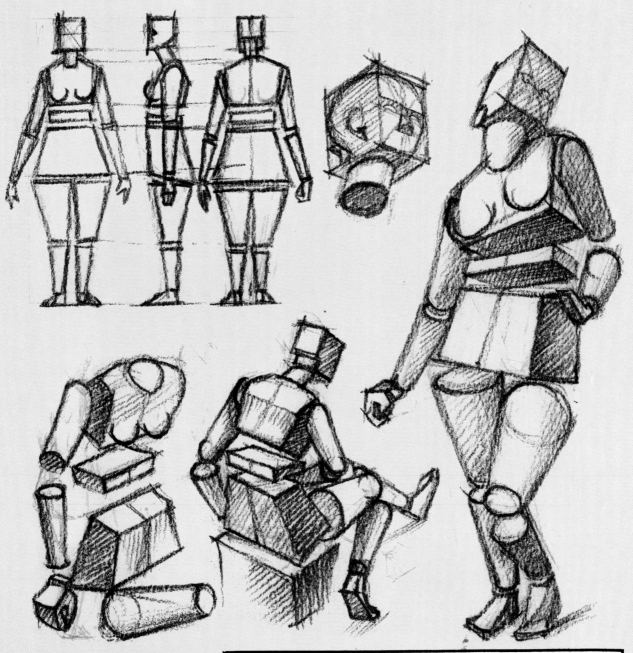

representing the head, neck, and limbs. It is useful to practise bending and twisting these blocks, bearing in mind the drawings on the previous page. In this way, the figure will reveal itself as being solid from the outset, and this conception of the figure as a series of simple masses is invaluable in constructing imaginary figures seen from different eye levels and viewpoints.

There are obvious differences in proportions of height, width, and mass between male and female forms as shown here.

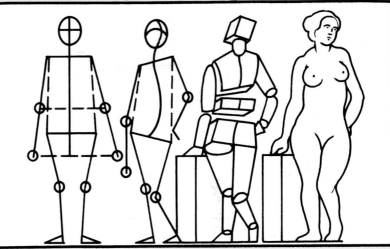

Using line

If we draw an outline of a disk viewed from above, we produce a circle as in figure 1, but as we look at the disk from various eye levels as a series of side views, we see that the shapes become ellipses as in figure 2. By strengthening the line of the edge of the disk that is nearest to us, we can "read" more successfully whether the disk is above or below our eye level.

Describing solid form

If we wish to represent solid form with line, then we have to make our line express other things besides just outline shape. By projecting the ellipses onto the circle, we can see that solid form is made up of horizontal and vertical sections through the circle (figure 3).

Now imagine the outline shape of a section through the human head (or what we would see as the silhouette of a shadow cast on a wall), as in figure 4. Keeping this same section of the head in mind, turn the head around until it is in a three-quarter position as in figure 5, and the edge of the imaginary section would form a line down the front centre of the head, over the top and down the opposite side. This would now reflect the form or "terrain" of the head as seen from a perspective viewpoint. This line, and particularly the part of it following the undulating form of the face, is called a *contour*.

Sections can also be imagined as though cut horizontally through the form (figures 6 and 7), and it is very important to be aware of the form right through and around the back and not just in the visible portion of the figure. This technique helps us to understand, and therefore express accurately, the whole solid form through a network of contour lines. Even when drawing from a single viewpoint, it is important to view the model from other positions to understand the form "in the round."

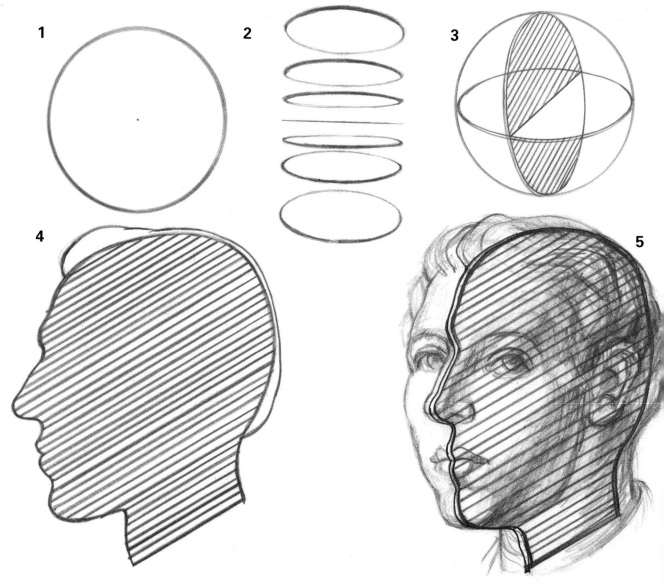

6

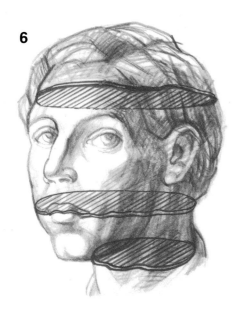

7

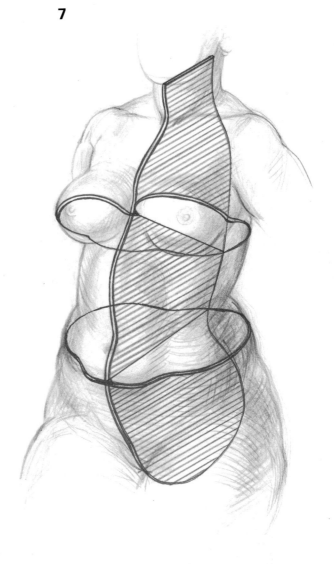

Understanding symmetry

With symmetrical forms like the human head, the outline of a cheek bone or temple is directly opposite the other in perspective, which, although not seen as outline, must be expressed as contour. Even if the other portion is not actually drawn, it must be imagined in the correct position. This accurate placing applies to the corners of the eyes, nostrils, and mouth (figure 8). An imaginary centre contour line running down the head is vital, and a series of section lines

8

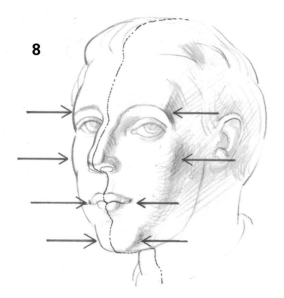

9

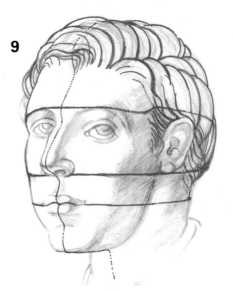

across the head will help considerably. In a line drawing, the main lines of the hair growth can act as contour lines describing the form (figure 9, Page 109).

Contours and volume

When viewing a cylindrical form as in figure 1, the vertical outlines should describe the points on either side where the curving surface disappears behind the mass. This point is shown clearly by drawing the elliptical section and the lines of sight running from the artist's eye to the very edge of the cylinder.

When our eye level is halfway between the top and the bottom (figure 2), we can only describe the ends of the cylinder by curved lines indicating the near edges of the cylinder top and bottom before the surface curves out of sight. Great care must be taken, therefore, to observe exactly where this turning away takes place. The effectiveness of the drawn outline and contour depends on how well we observe the section or "turn" of the form from its nearest point to us and should give the feeling of continuing around behind the form.

Assessing the human form

The volumes of the figure are rarely, if ever, perfectly circular or cylindrical. They range from nearly boxlike to ovoid or nearly circular. For example, if we feel the section of our own wrists, we will feel that it is a flattened, box-like form compared with a rounder ovoid form further up the lower arm. It is wrong to use circular contour lines unless representative of the form.

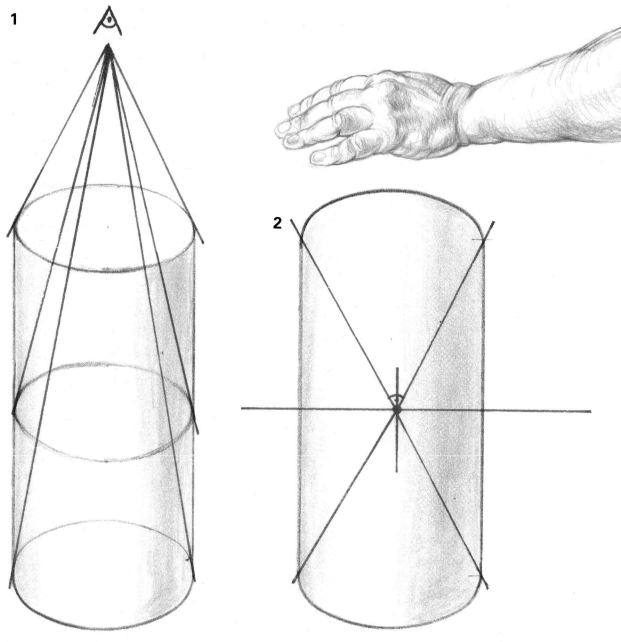

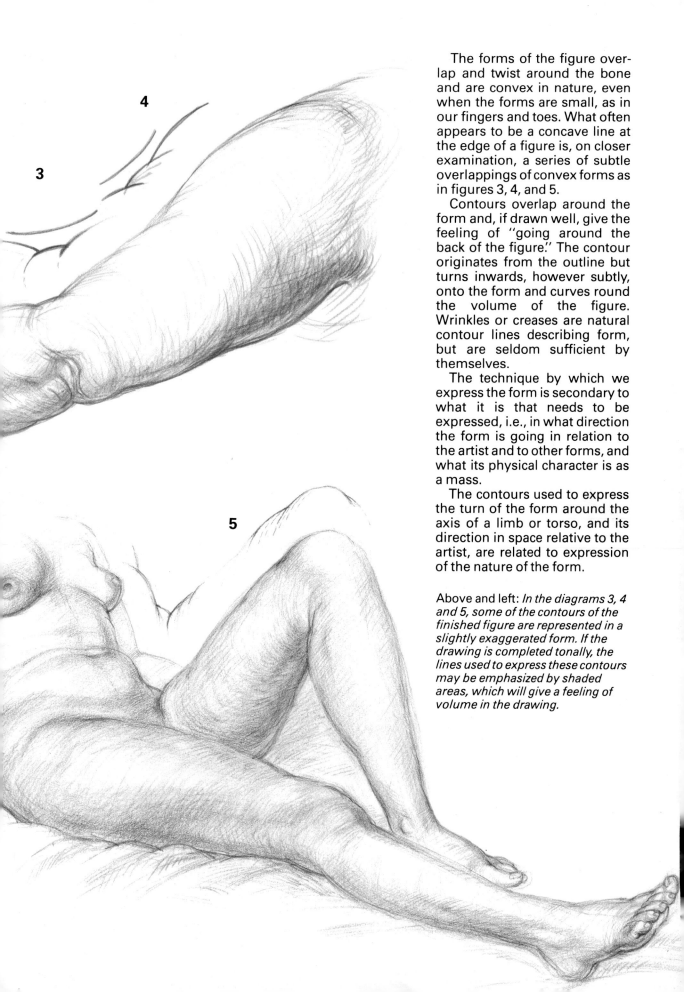

4

3

5

The forms of the figure overlap and twist around the bone and are convex in nature, even when the forms are small, as in our fingers and toes. What often appears to be a concave line at the edge of a figure is, on closer examination, a series of subtle overlappings of convex forms as in figures 3, 4, and 5.

Contours overlap around the form and, if drawn well, give the feeling of "going around the back of the figure." The contour originates from the outline but turns inwards, however subtly, onto the form and curves round the volume of the figure. Wrinkles or creases are natural contour lines describing form, but are seldom sufficient by themselves.

The technique by which we express the form is secondary to what it is that needs to be expressed, i.e., in what direction the form is going in relation to the artist and to other forms, and what its physical character is as a mass.

The contours used to express the turn of the form around the axis of a limb or torso, and its direction in space relative to the artist, are related to expression of the nature of the form.

Above and left: *In the diagrams 3, 4 and 5, some of the contours of the finished figure are represented in a slightly exaggerated form. If the drawing is completed tonally, the lines used to express these contours may be emphasized by shaded areas, which will give a feeling of volume in the drawing.*

1

Contour drawing

The main directions of the volumes in the drawing below are shown by the accompanying diagrams of sections through the form. Many forms are partly hidden from view by those in front, so think of the contours going behind and being overlapped by those in front, as we would draw a distant range of hills in a landscape. See figures 1 and 2. It will help to think of the shape of the human figure as being analogous to the terrain of a landscape.

The contours used in expressing the turn of the form should be drawn with reference to the light and dark areas as the form turns to and from the light source. The contours will appear

Left: *The full, rich forms of rocks, hills and clouds are expressed by overlapping contours in a landscape drawing.*

Below: *In reality, the contours of the nude figure are much more subtle than in the diagram opposite.*

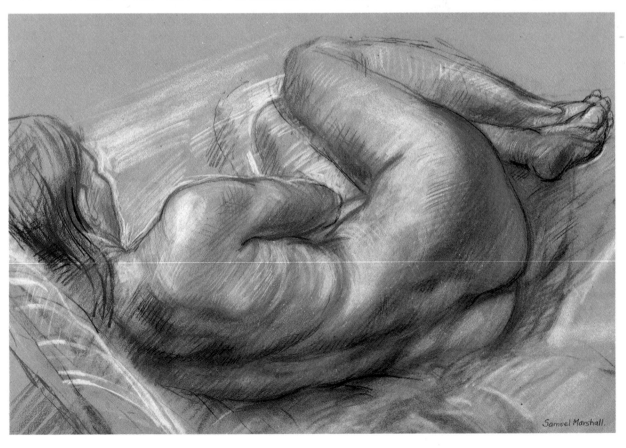

Samuel Marshall.

darker as they curve away from the light, but a complete tonal rendition should be left to a drawing in charcoal, chalk, or paint. Contour drawings select from the whole range of tones only those which are needed to "turn" and describe the form. Very often the darkest tone is not the edge of the form but where the major plane of the front turns around to the side plane.

Contour drawing can become a very personal visual language, differing from artist to artist. The lines in a Dürer engraving, for example, are very different from those in the pen drawings of Rubens, Michaelangelo, or Raphael. It is worth making accurate copies of some of these with a view to understanding the artist's use of line.

2

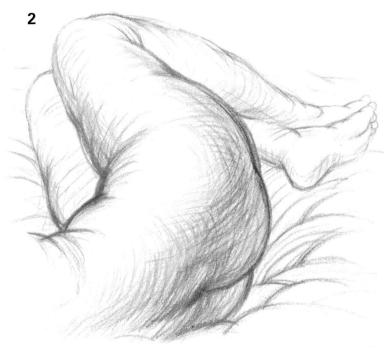

Above right: *The human figure can be expressed by overlapping contours, as in landscape forms.*

Below: *Varying sections, with contour lines and showing the axial direction, through parts selected from the drawing opposite.*

Right: *This shows the difference between outline and contour in expressing sections through form. In a) the outline does not convey the volume or direction of the bottle. In b) the label acts as a contour, explaining both the section through volume and the direction.*

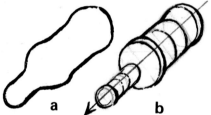

a   b

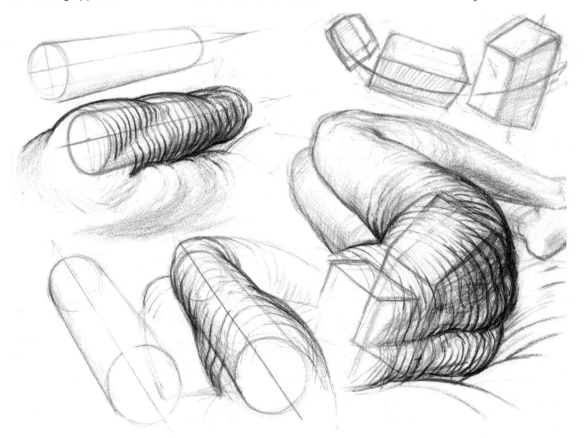

Proportion

In observing people around us, we see a great variety of differences in figure proportions, and this variety is important to the accuracy of a drawing. There is, however, a fairly widely accepted "norm" or average from which deviations such as "fat" or "thin" occur. This standard will be only a basic guide, but it does give the artist some point of reference for assessing more individual figures.

The drawings on this page show how the figure can be described by a circle, and by a triangle. This is apparent when we look at a figure from an undistorted viewpoint.

However, many viewpoints involve foreshortening of the head, torso, limbs, and the actual observed proportions of the body are seen to change radically.

When faced with this problem, it is important to remember that we are drawing a normal human figure and that the

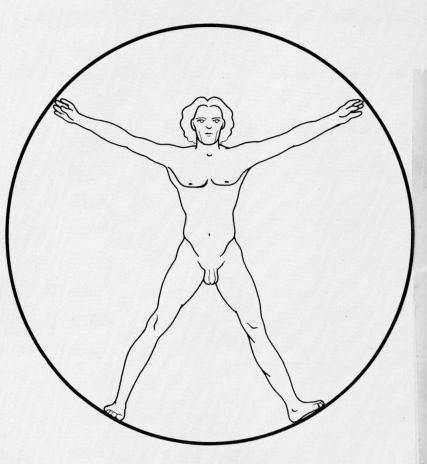

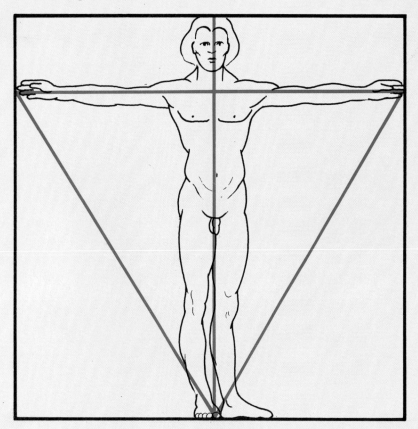

Above and left: *These illustrations are based on Leonardo da Vinci's theories of proportion and represent ideals which may be considered a synthesis of many differing proportions. They are useful as a starting point from which to observe the variety of ways in which individuals differ.*

distortions are not deformities. Foreshortening is a product of perspective and will affect the box-structure of the masses that describe the figure.

Proportions of the head

The side view of the head, from the top of the skull to the chin and from the tip of the nose to the back of the skull, is basically a square. The total width across the skull goes into the total height about one and a half times. The hair is an extra layer or mass on top of this.

The head, even in the smoother female form, should

be shown to have a front, side, top, bottom, and back plane. A vertical line down the middle may be used, and horizontal proportion lines for the features should be placed at one-third intervals: the first placed at the level of the line of the eyebrows, the second on a level with the base of the nose.

The top of the ear is level with the eyebrows and the bottom with the nostril. The mouth is halfway between the chin and nose and the eyes are an eye-width apart. These proportions describe the standard adult. Children have smaller faces in proportion to their skulls.

Right: *These two diagrams show how perspective alters our perception of a box and a figure and provides an elementary aid to drawing foreshortened or "end-on" subjects.*

Below: *When drawing a face or head, it is essential to fix the basic proportions first. These are the height and the width, and from here they can be broken down as shown below. Here the main features divide the face up into thirds but remember that the proportions will alter visually from different viewpoints.*

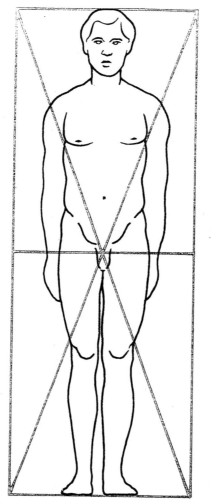

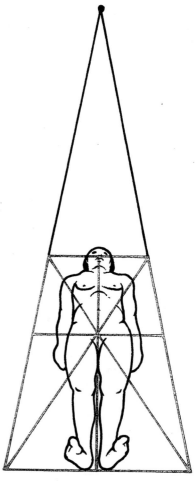

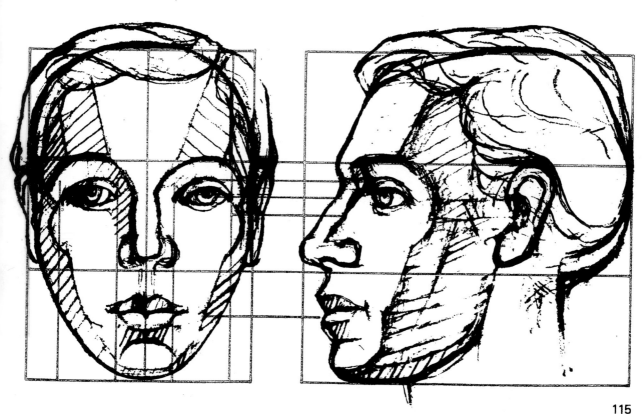

Recording detail

The masses, or block forms, of the hands and feet are governed by the bone structure.

Hands

In the hand, apart from the rounder masses of the ball of the thumb and the palm, the planes are angular and well defined. Construction lines should be used to help locate the key points.

The block-line form of the lower arm joins the bones of wrist and palm which make one important block with a clearly defined plane, i.e., the back of the hand which is large and slightly convex. A small plane runs down the outside to the first joint of the little finger. On the thumb side there is a larger, wedge-shaped plane.

The line of the knuckles is extremely important, as they define the major changes of the planes of the fingers. The bones of the fingers are squarish in section, particularly at the knuckles.

Below: *Many people are convinced that a hand is too difficult to draw; it may help to think of it in terms of a form or block.*

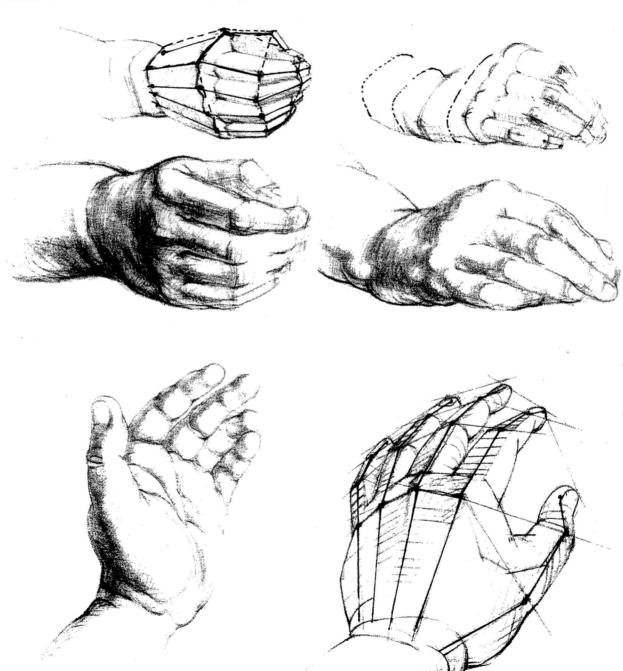

116

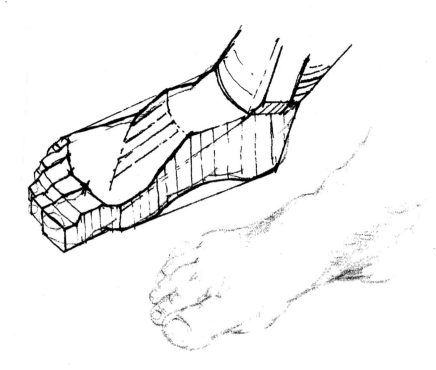

Left: *Look at the skeleton to establish the inner axial direction of the bones, as the form of the foot is governed by its bone structure.*

Below: *Feet and hands can both be considered as miniature "landscapes" of planes and forms. From the block form you must then evolve a more rounded and flowing natural line. Also consider the form of the foot when extended.*

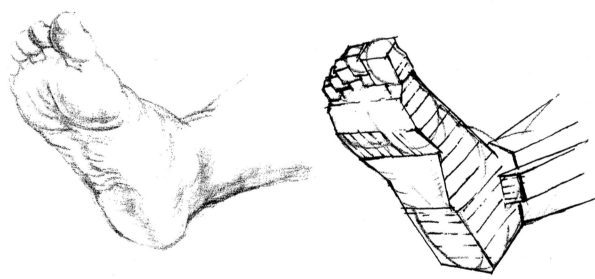

Feet

In drawing the foot, as with the hand, the bone structure has a very obvious influence on the block form. In contrast to the wrist, the comparable bone mass in the foot, the tarsals, meets the shaft of the ankle at right angles where they fit into a joint, as in the wrist and lower arm, and allow for considerable movement. The inner joint of the

ankle is higher than the outer and this influences the outward and downward tilt of the top plane of the instep towards the toes. The high ridge running down to the big toe marks the major change of plane from top to side plane.

The inner-side plane then curves underneath to allow for the arch of the foot between the squarish mass of the heel and the ball of the foot at the toe end.

The toes themselves are smaller, squarish blocks, starting with the larger mass of the big toe and diminishing to the little toe. The latter also marks the end of the important bevel or outside plane of the foot, just as the little finger marks that of the hand. Again, use construction lines to establish main points, remembering that, like the hand, the foot can be flexed or extended.

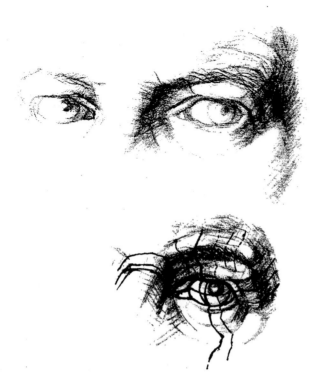

Although the features of the face are small, they are very important and a consideration of the planes will help when drawing them. The features are studied separately here, but you should always bear in mind their relation to the whole head.

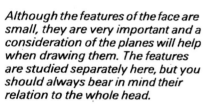

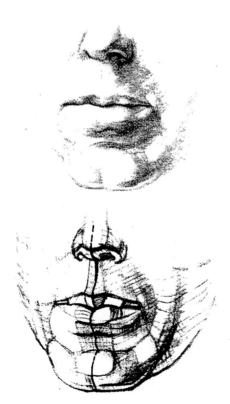

Eyes

The eye is a ball set into a socket or recess in the front of the face. The beginning of the top plane of the socket is marked by the eyebrows, and the inside plane is a continuation of the upper-side plane of the nose. The outside and lower planes are the projections of the cheekbones. The upper eyelid slides up and down over the eyeball, while the lower one remains almost stationary.

Lips

The fullness of the lips projecting from the front plane of the face is governed to some degree by the curvature of the teeth behind them. The upper lip starts below the nose with a small groove or wedge-shaped centre, flanked by planes tapering to the corners of the mouth. The lower lip overhangs a plane sloping back to the ball of the chin, and the surface divides into two rounded forms that meet in a slight depression. In most cases, the lower lip is fuller than the upper lip.

Nose

The basic form of the nose is a wedge-shaped mass arising from the frontal plane of the face. Its front plane starts just under the forehead and separates the two eye sockets. The top part is narrow and bony; the lower part is cartilage and forms the central "bulb" between the two nostrils. The latter, though curved, lie on the two wedge-shaped side planes and their bases form a flat plane.

Ears

The ears tend to slant inwards and downwards, parallel to the cheeks, and can be divided into thirds from top to bottom. The centre is the "bowl," the lower third is the lobe, and the upper is the curling rim of the ear. These forms, although small, are fully modelled and twisting in character, not flat. The back view shows a shallow "trumpet." The ear and nose are on a level and are the same depth.

Hair

It is important to regard hair also as a mass. Although its soft texture and our awareness that it is composed of separate strands makes this difficult, the hair should be thought of as an extra layer over the skull. Sometimes the hair lies very close to the skull and accentuates the form, while at other times, though lying close to the skull at the top, it can break away to form block forms of its own. The linear movement of the growth of hair within the mass should help to describe the form.

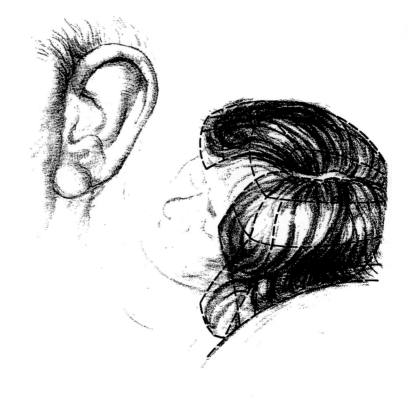

Above: *The broken diagrammatic lines on the nose show the underlying essential wedge-block form on which the more subtle forms are built.*

Right: *When drawing hair, try to avoid superficially copying its appearance. Use the basic planes shown here so that the natural movement of the hair can be represented.*

Tackling a subject

The drawings reproduced in the next few pages contain many of the factors discussed so far. The illustrations will examine these factors in more detail.

Figure 1 illustrates the position and direction of movement of the main axial-skeletal structure of the human figure; this is the framework on which everything else is built.

Figure 2 illustrates the layout of the main block masses of the figure. The influence of the laws of perspective is important and must be considered when approaching this kind of subject.

Figure 3 illustrates the positions of overlapping contours which help to express the form of the figure and develop it from a hard, two-dimensional outline.

Figure 4 analyzes the main areas of light and shade which are used in the drawing to help represent solid form, and to create an interesting composition.

The head in the main drawing illustrates some of the points discussed earlier:

a) The artist was seated at a lower eye level than the model, so he had to give a feeling of looking up at the head. Perspective is again important here.

b) The proportions of the head were modified by this low eye level, so that care had to be taken to make the head appear normal rather than distorted.

c) The light, coming from the right front, models the major change of planes by creating areas of light and dark in which the minor plane alterations are shown by the use of halftones and reflected lights.

d) The hair is treated as a mass lying over the skull. Some lines are used to indicate the direction of growth of the hair.

The details of features are also conceived as block masses

1

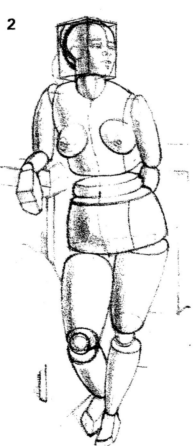

Above: *In this diagrammatic representation, direction is summed up with one line. Note the contrasting angles through the shoulders and pelvis, and the foreshortening in the fore-arm. The red vertical line represents the line of gravity, obtained by a plumbline to give the correct stance.*

Below: *This does not represent a style of drawing, but rather a way of thinking. Lightly sketching in these block forms may help you to see how their underlying direction governs everything else (see also pages 106 and 107). Notice here the very different direction of the volume of the head and the pelvis.*

2

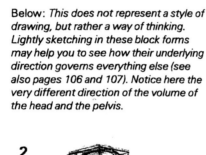

3

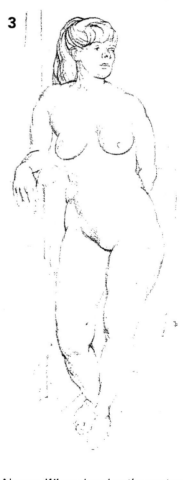

Above: *When drawing the contours of the figure, bear in mind the areas of light and dark. This includes the background lighting as well, and the effect that this has upon the figure. The contours of the figure will be highlighted or in shadow, according to the light, and the background need not be clearly defined.*

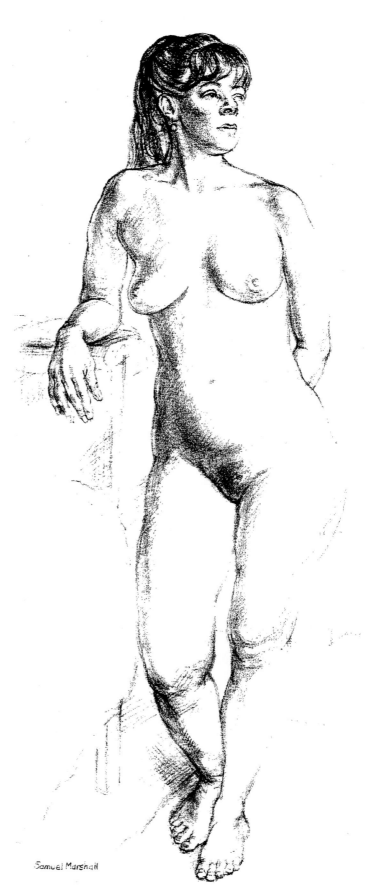

which receive the same light as the underlying major plane.

Although in the analytical diagrams accompanying the drawing on page 122 the first stage is shown as being the plotting of main directions in the figure, it is not always necessary to draw in line first, with tone added later. The driving force behind your wish to make a drawing should be your emotional reaction to the subject, and this will affect your choice of technique.

Above: *The amount of light and shade in drawings varies according to the pictorial idea to be expressed. Here it is used mainly in the figure to express form.*

Right: *In the finished drawing, as the chief aim is the study of the form of the figure, the background tones are kept to a minimum and a small amount of line and tone is used to create a sense of space around the figure. In a drawing with dramatic use of lighting to enhance the subject, there would be more use of background line and tone.*

Samuel Marshall

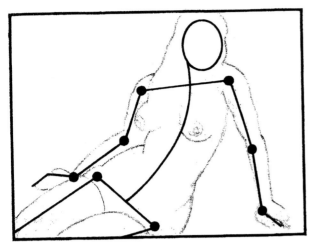 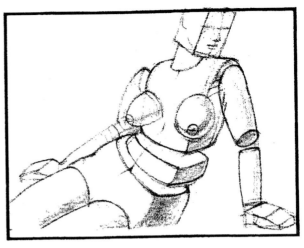

The first drawing above shows the main axial-skeletal lines superimposed onto the silhouette of the figure. These lines, as shown previously, are the basis for any figure drawing; their weight has been exaggerated here for clarity.

When beginning a drawing, keep the lines light and be ready to adjust them where necessary. If the proportions are shown correctly at this stage you will be able to concentrate later on describing form and the play of light and shade.

The second drawing shows the logical progression to form; in your studies this will be added over the top of the lightly drawn axis lines and should itself remain light in its handling. This will be refined to result in the drawing shown below.

In this drawing the medium used was conté crayon, the main angles and directions providing the motivating force in the composition. The volumes interacted in a rhythmic way and the block forms, or combination of box and cylinder, echoed through this drawing right down to the fingers.

The adult and child study on this page was started with charcoal to establish the main masses of light and dark. This was then fixed and greater definition added with conté crayon. The design and composition of the two figures were considered extremely important, the direction of the angles of limbs, torso, and head giving an integrated and dynamic design. The large areas were blocked in before working on details of the head and hands, and the direction of the light was important in showing the relief of the forms. The characteristics of both the adult and child forms and proportions were essential for this drawing.

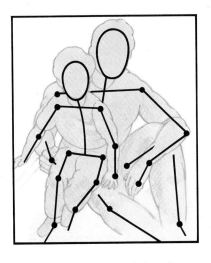

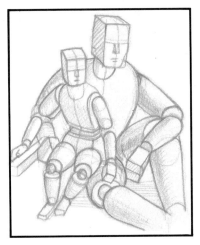

Using charcoal, a fluid medium which is easily removed, begin the drawing with the indication of direction of form (more lightly than is shown here). Once the proportion is considered to be correct start the drawing in earnest, defining the form in a general way.

The block form shown in the second stage drawing is useful as a means by which to define the proportions and weight of the figures. If the form is drawn too wide, the figure will appear to be fat and must be trimmed down. This should be done at this stage; it will be more difficult to correct if left until later.

Alterations are now made to the basic block form of the figures to give them the appearance of specific figures as opposed to general human shapes.

Work at all times as generally as possible and do not be in too much of a hurry to draw in the detail before the form is consolidated. A generalized drawing which really appears to have solidity and weight and appears to exist in space is far more desirable than a highly detailed study which appears flat. While working do not be afraid to make alterations even if they appear to be drastic. By modifying a drawing in the light of error a more lively result is often obtained. The best drawings are the result of a continual process of refinement.

The clothed figure

The crucial factor in drawing the clothed figure is that it has a solid body beneath the clothing. Simply copying surface effects, and painstakingly representing every fold, will not necessarily produce this impression. We have to look for the areas where the body masses support the clothing and thus reveal themselves at the surface, and it is at this point that the understanding of the "blocks" of the figure's volume becomes really important.

In a standing figure, the main areas of support for the clothes are the shoulders and the waist. When the figure bends or sits, other portions become the supports. A useful clue to the nature of folds is to observe a piece of cloth hanging on a line when the folds radiate out from the points of support.

The drawing of two seated figures (opposite) shows how the major planes of the underlying forms affect the surface form of the clothing, and how actions like the man's forward-extended right arm and leg create folds which radiate out from the point of support. When properly observed and drawn they help to express the form by the way in which they twist around it.

The expression of form in the woman's left shoulder is helped by the folds caused by her left arm pressing against the upper torso. Notice the broad planes of her back beneath the clothing, and the large folds of her dress pulling from the top plane of her thigh.

Below: *The figures here clearly show how the form beneath acts as a support for the clothing. The light areas indicate the points of support, where the clothing clings more closely: the shoulders, breasts and across the hips. On the seated figure, it also clings to the thigh and upper leg. Notice also how parts of the hair mass echo the underlying form of the skull and reveal its shape, particularly on the crown of the head.*

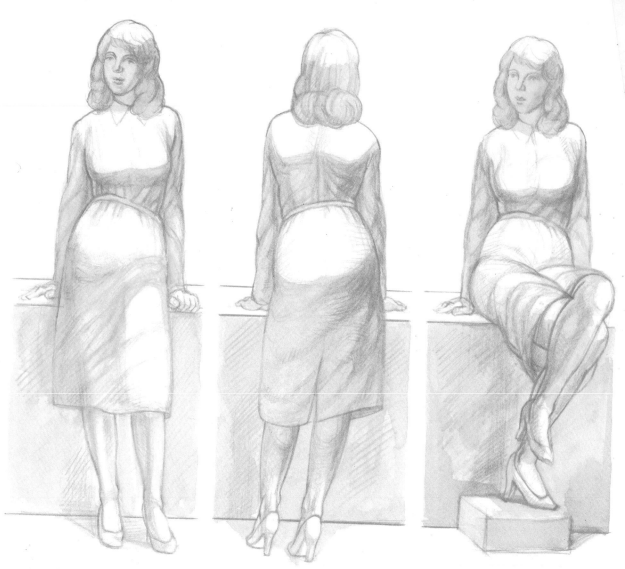

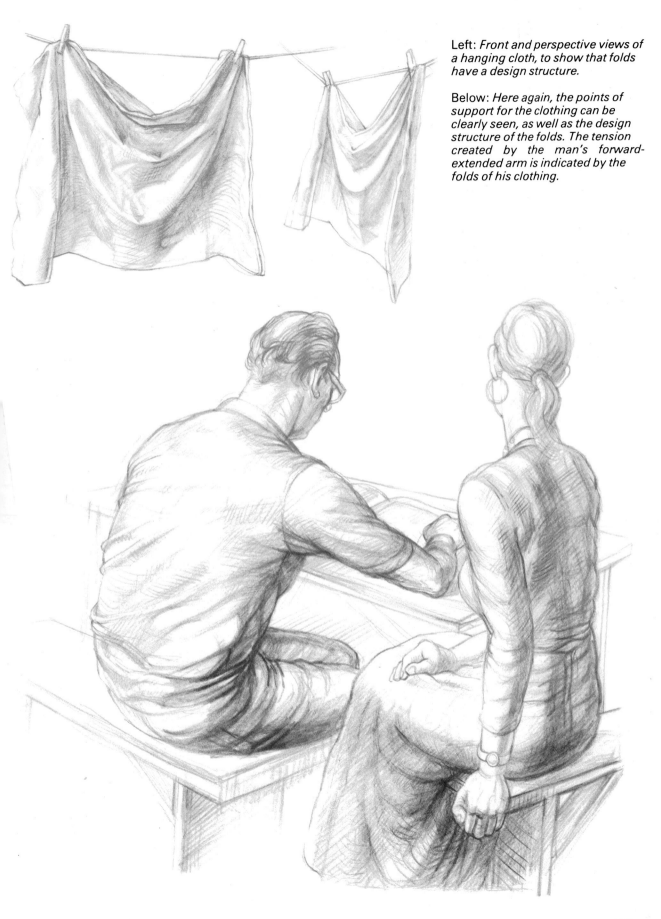

Left: *Front and perspective views of a hanging cloth, to show that folds have a design structure.*

Below: *Here again, the points of support for the clothing can be clearly seen, as well as the design structure of the folds. The tension created by the man's forward-extended arm is indicated by the folds of his clothing.*

125

Expressing volume

As the basic forms of trouser legs or sleeves and the body of shirts or blouses are fundamentally cylindrical, their ends or seams can help to describe the form of the figure (figure 1). Some lines going round the form, like a watchstrap around a wrist (figure 2) are comparatively tight, and so describe the "section" of the figure very clearly. This can also happen on closely worn clothing, like a shirt collar and tie (figure 6) or a roll-neck sweater (figure 4), and they are very useful for expressing the three-dimensional quality.

Other clothing which is fairly loosely worn, though not lying close to the form, can still help to express volume. Sometimes part of an edge of a sleeve or hem of a dress can lie close to the figure to provide a contour. Lines made by clothing which run down the body are just as useful in describing the figure, if only by describing the middle line (figure 3).

Pattern in clothing can assist greatly in reflecting the "terrain" of the form; stripes can act as ready-made contours. Stripes and patterns should always be drawn with an eye to the form, whether in line or tone. Notice, for instance, how the distance between stripes seems to diminish as they approach the edges of the form before disappearing around the back (figure 4).

Think of hats and caps as being projections of the skull. The brim should help to express the form of the head as it passes around the forehead and sides (figures 5 and 7).

1

2

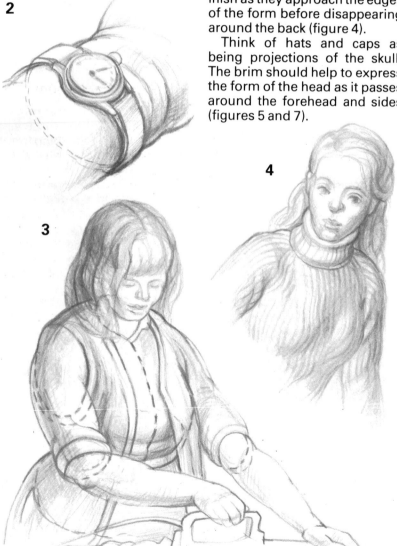

5

4

3

Above, left and opposite: Virtually anything that encircles a body, from a wrist watch to the neck of a sweater, can be used to define the form beneath. Keep in mind that materials vary in the way in which they react to movement. Consider the folds of clothing carefully – they can give life to a drawing or destroy its reality depending upon their positioning and they way in which they are drawn.

6

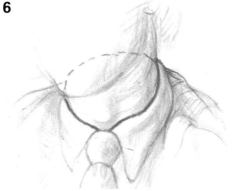

Above: *This sketch illustrates the visualization of form and volume. The concept must be kept in mind at all times while drawing or the results will look flat and unconvincing.*

Right: *In this figure study, the head and hat are more highly finished than the rest of the figure. The body retains its solidity, however, because the form was considered from the outset.*

7

8

Expressing movement

In vigorous action, the movement of folds and the thrusting outwards of the underlying form is much more accentuated than in a static figure (figure 8). Start by blocking in the direction lines and volumes of the body, and then draw the main movements of folds over the top. With practice in observing the direction and design of folds, imaginative figures can be constructed convincingly.

Try making observational drawings of figures in movement in your sketchbook continually, as this will teach you to grasp the essentials of movement quickly. Then build up these figures more completely from memory, trying to retain the important planes and folds.

Finally, the characteristic quality of certain kinds of clothing materials influences the extent to which the form is revealed. Stiff materials tend to wrinkle in an angular way and they resist movement somewhat. Soft, light materials, such as silk, show the underlying form more clearly.

Sketching

Whether or not your main interest is in drawing posed subjects, you should devote as much time as possible to working from the world at large. Firstly, working from the posed model, though essential for learning the basic language of forms, is artificial by nature, and can result in the acquisition of drawing "habits," styles, and mannerisms. We tend to select the same viewpoints or those safely within our known abilities.

Everybody needs the vigorous and invigorating unpredict-ability of everyday life to stretch their capabilities. There is little time to worry about style when drawing moving figures and, in striving to capture the key lines, masses, and tones, we have to shed many of our preconceptions and visual inhibitions.

Finding a subject

To start with, however, it is advisable to select subjects that are not so ambitious that the novice will become discouraged, and to make a number of swift studies before tackling another subject. Alternatively, keep returning to favourite themes with both quick and more highly finished drawings from as many different viewpoints as possible. Do not worry about the drawings having the same degree of accuracy as would be achieved with a posed subject, but search for other qualities, such as economy of line or expressive pattern of form.

It is not necessary to travel far to find suitable subjects for sketching; family, friends, and your immediate environment offer excellent opportunities for characterization, movement, and action. Always try to capture people in natural situations such as sewing, cooking, playing games, and so on.

Below: *This linear drawing, with soft pencil, was caught in about ten minutes, just before bedtime. Notice the girl's posture, and her air of reverie.*

Opposite above: *A tonal drawing, with the tonal area emphasized quickly and boldly with a soft pencil, as the lighting was important. Again, notice how the posture has been caught.*

Opposite below: *A sheet from a sketchbook. Babies are a good subject for sketching practice; you must be quick and bold and ready to catch their movements.*

Learn from sketching

An important function of sketching is to explore the limits of your technical abilities, as well as to learn more of the nature of forms. False starts, failures, various "scribbles" are all natural components in a growing sketchbook, and all have a contribution of some kind to make. Decisions and execution should always be swiftly made, with emphasis placed more on the instinctively felt angles across shoulders and hips, the axial directions of limbs and torso, the sway of a garment against the tension and relaxation of underlying muscles. There is no time for slow, deliberate appraisal of proportion or outline, and the mind must work faster than the hand. Try to work unnoticed as much as possible. This will minimize self-consciousness in both your subject and yourself. You can often work inconspicuously from hidden vantage points or from behind an open newspaper in a train, bus, or café.

Avoid flicking your eyes

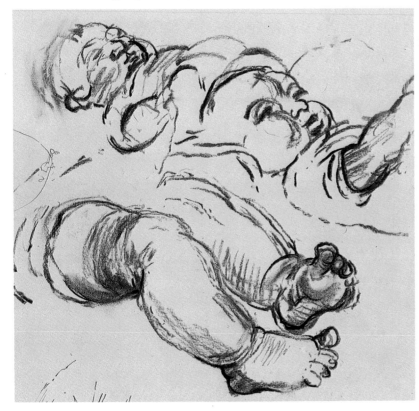

rapidly from subject to drawing pad, as this will attract attention as well as interrupt your own concentration. Take long, infrequent looks, committing your subject to memory before drawing. This will also help to develop your visual memory. Aim for a certain number of sketchbook drawings per week and be ambitious. One hundred would not be too many when most of them will be quick sketches.

The materials for sketching are simple. There are many makes of sketchpads on the market, in a variety of sizes. Even if you like working on a large scale, select a small pad which can be carried in pocket or handbag in addition. Experiment and use a range of materials: pencils, charcoal, inks, and chalks. Choose materials which you can easily carry in a box or cloth roll.

Advanced techniques

There are many instances in drawing where what we want to express demands a direct fluency and variety of line which a pencil is unable to give. The possibilities of linear variety with pen or brush and ink are wide-ranging; a stylus or technical drawing pen produces a delicate but unvarying line, felt-tipped pens can range from thick to thin, dip pens can produce a sensitive line varying from thin to broad, according to the degree of pressure.

Try making lines in all these media, including charcoal and pastel, on different papers to get the feel of them. Make a mental note of their diverse expressive qualities. A thick, jagged line, for example, is very rich and powerful and can impart emphasis and solidity to a drawing. In contrast, smooth, curving lines can suggest elegance and a subtle sensuality.

Different thicknesses of line in a drawing are very desirable, as they can impart a feeling of depth and space. For example, if the seated model's knee near the artist is drawn heavily and with emphasis in relation to the lighter linear drawing in the torso behind the leg, the line will create the feeling of the knee coming forward from the torso.

In addition, empathy plays a vital role: variety of line is something which comes naturally if we physically "feel" what the model is doing, almost as though we are "acting" the pose in sympathy. A model may be supporting her whole body weight on one leg, the other being very relaxed, for instance. If we enact this to ourselves, we should feel the line biting into the paper with great emphasis when drawing the supporting leg, as opposed to the quieter line made for the other leg. This empathy is just as important in drawing planes and volumes.

Sometimes a line is not sufficient even in a quick, direct sketch. Pen and wash has long been a medium for swift and economical statements of form: Rembrandt was one of its greatest exponents. With a few strongly felt, but carefully selected, strokes of the brush, planes, volume, and atmosphere can all be suggested to lend substance to a line drawing. It can also be used to contribute atmosphere to charcoal and conté drawings.

Wash and watercolour drawing requires some practice in laying down areas of wash and gradated tone in order to familiarize yourself with the inherent quality and directness of the medium, but the results can be well worth the effort.

Below: *This drawing with a soft pencil illustrates the use of a variety of smooth curving lines to help express the languorous pose.*

Left: *This detail shows the use of mixed media, including charcoal, pastel and some gouache. It is a complete, imaginative figure composition, inspired mainly from memory. The thickness of the line on the foreground figures is made much heavier and more angular by the use of a brush and chalk, to help express the volume. This is in contrast with the more dreamlike figures in the background. The original is a large scale drawing, which started with charcoal and gradually built up to paint to acquire definition.*

Below: *This is a brush drawing using a watercolour wash technique. No preliminary drawing was made and the emphasis is on the calligraphic handling of the brush, to just suggest the body and the hair. The background is hardly defined at all and the design and atmosphere of the drawing culminates in the head, where the face is slightly in shadow.*

ANIMALS
Introduction to anatomy

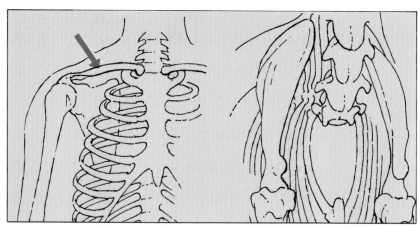

You are not expected to memorize the position and name of every bone in an animal's skeleton. However, if you take animal drawing seriously, you should understand what underlies the exterior form and which positions or movements are physically possible. The most important features of the skeleton are common to many vertebrates, including man, and they share the same names.

The most obvious difference between the four-legged animal and man is the design of the leg and foot bones. Most animals walk on their toes with their "heel" and "wrist" held high off the ground. The horse, for example, walks on only one toe, the others having atrophied.

Another important difference is the lack of a developed collar bone (arrowed) – although it is present in some climbing animals like the squirrel. The horse's foreleg is attached to its body only by a muscle, but this is able to absorb a great deal of concussion that would otherwise be transmitted to the spine.

Nearly all animals, including man, have seven vertebrae in the neck. The size and flexibility varies according to the animal's feeding habits. Similarly, the number of dorsal and lumbar

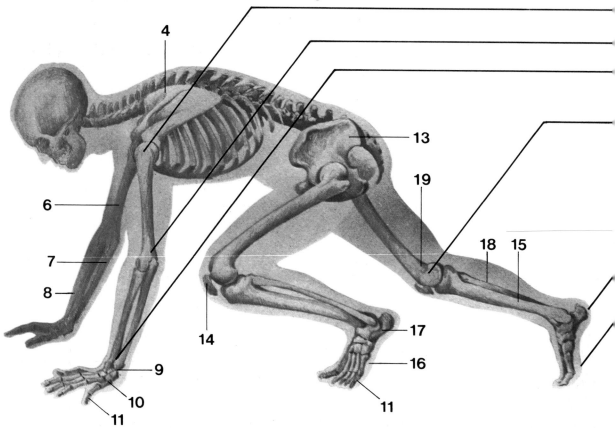

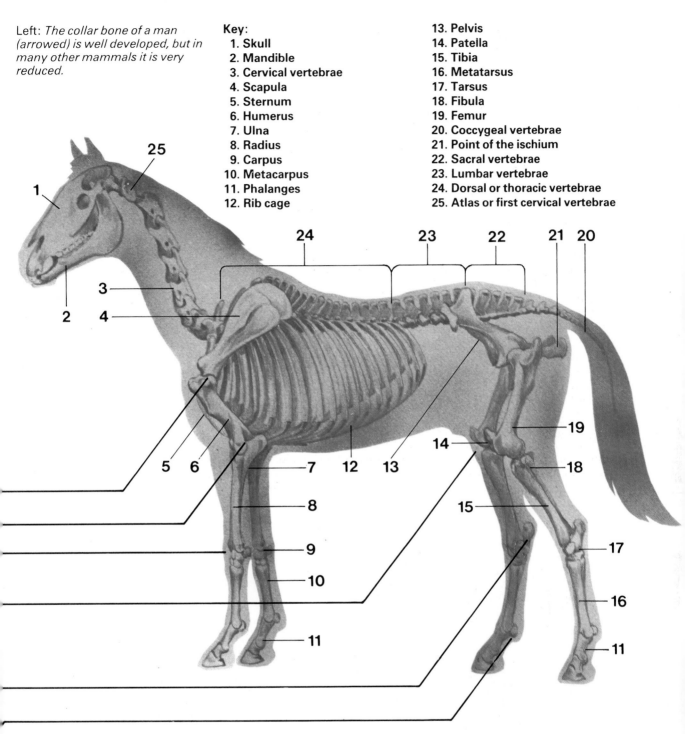

Left: *The collar bone of a man (arrowed) is well developed, but in many other mammals it is very reduced.*

Key:
1. Skull
2. Mandible
3. Cervical vertebrae
4. Scapula
5. Sternum
6. Humerus
7. Ulna
8. Radius
9. Carpus
10. Metacarpus
11. Phalanges
12. Rib cage
13. Pelvis
14. Patella
15. Tibia
16. Metatarsus
17. Tarsus
18. Fibula
19. Femur
20. Coccygeal vertebrae
21. Point of the ischium
22. Sacral vertebrae
23. Lumbar vertebrae
24. Dorsal or thoracic vertebrae
25. Atlas or first cervical vertebrae

Left and above: *Comparison of the skeletal structure of a man with that of a horse.*

vertebrae in the spine are about the same but they, too, vary in size and shape, giving the characteristic back contour of each species. Lateral movement in the lumbar vertebrae (our waist) is very much restricted in a horse, but a carnivore like the cat can twist its body easily. The position and shape of the pelvis also varies a great deal (compare the pelvis of a man to that of a horse). Similarly, the skull is noticeably different and has developed according to the animal's feeding habits (compare a cat's skull to the horse's skull). Notice also, particularly in the case of a man, the relative area occupied by the brain.

In the following chapters about the basic structures of the dog, cat and horse you will be introduced to the main points of the structure of each animal's skeleton. The same applies to the chapters dealing with form. These chapters are intended to help you to construct your drawings by providing information which is not immediately visible in your subject.

Dogs: basic structure

Dogs, particularly large short-haired varieties like the labrador, are ideal subjects for studying animal anatomy. As you are drawing, imagine the skeleton underlying the hair and muscle and try to identify some of the main bones and joints.

There is little doubt that the domestic dog is related to the wolf and jackal. The skeleton of a large dog is so similar to that of a wolf that it is difficult to tell them apart. The spine of a dog consists of seven vertebrae in the neck (cervical), thirteen in the back (dorsal or thoracic), seven in the loins (lumbar), three sacral and twenty to twenty-two in the tail (coccygeal). In both the

dog and the wolf there are thirteen pairs of ribs, and both animals have forty-two teeth. They also both have five front and four hind toes.

The shape and position of all these bones are illustrated by the skeleton below. However, take note of several "landmarks" which will be important in the drawing's construction.

If you can remember to look for these points you will be able to construct a very simple structure based on the skeleton. The drawings below show how this structure of lines works in a variety of positions. Look for the direction of the spine and the angle of the shoulders and haunches (pelvis). If these angles and proportions are judged badly, your drawing will be built upon an inaccurate foundation. It is vital to get that basic construction correct, so practise drawing just the lines

formed by the main bones of your subject and you will soon learn to "feel" when a drawing is correct.

Key:

1. The angle of the scapula **(shoulder blade).**

2. The protruding top end of the humerus (point of the shoulder).

3. The protruding top end of the ulna (point of the elbow).

4. The change in direction of the leg at the carpus (foreknee) which corresponds to the wrist in humans.

5. The joint of the metacarpus and the phalanges on the front and hind legs (ball of foot).

6. The back end of the tarsus **(heel).**

7. The joint of the femur and tibia.

8. The point of the ischium **(rounded back end of the pelvis).**

9. The joint of the femur with the pelvis.

10. The crest of the ilium (the front end of the pelvis).

11. The protruding wing of the atlas or first cervical vertebrae.

12. The back of the skull.

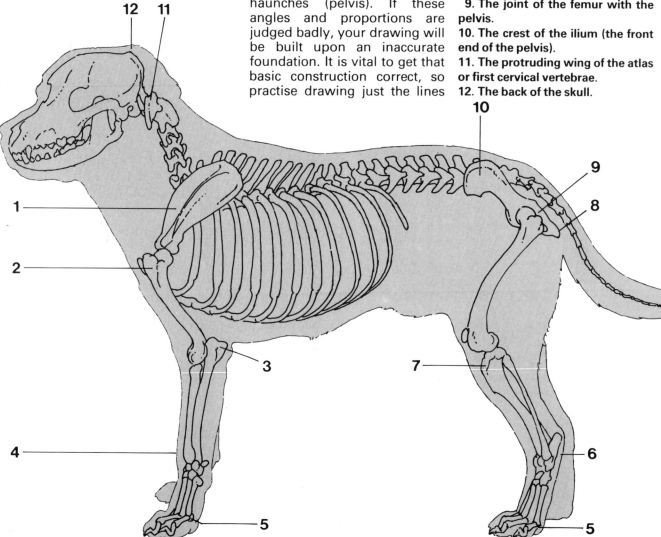

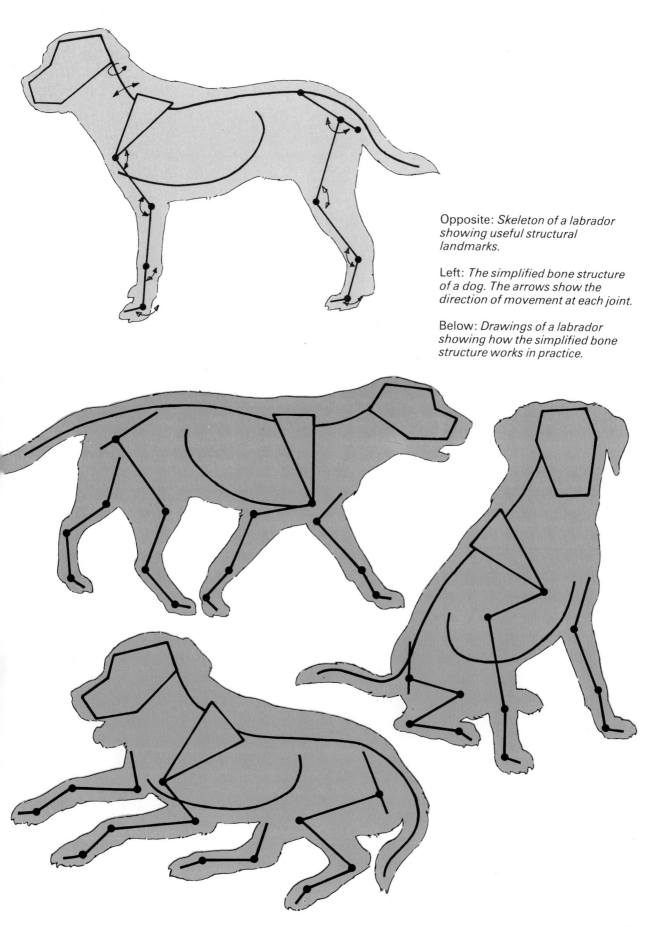

Opposite: *Skeleton of a labrador showing useful structural landmarks.*

Left: *The simplified bone structure of a dog. The arrows show the direction of movement at each joint.*

Below: *Drawings of a labrador showing how the simplified bone structure works in practice.*

Dogs: basic form

Left: *Detail of the leg muscles.*

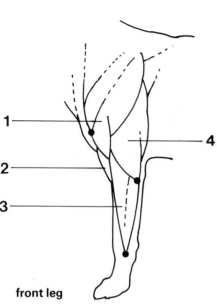

front leg

hind leg

The muscles and ligaments which control the movement of the bones produce a complex network of layers which create the form of the body. The shoulder, buttock (haunch) and leg muscles are particularly developed and I have drawn diagrams of these two areas to help you establish the main muscles. You should be able to identify them on the photograph. On the forelegs and hindlegs the muscles that are apparent on the surface are listed in the key.

In order to understand the formation of the muscles it is a good idea to visualize the body as simple, geometric volumes. As the drawing progresses sections can be added and cut away until a more natural form emerges. Try to visualize the surface as a pattern of planes or facets and you will find it easier to compare angles and shapes on the drawing with those of the subject. Use a pencil held at arm's length to compare lengths or angles.

We do not know when the dog first became domesticated, but man has certainly influenced the evolution of the large variety of breeds we find today. Some

Key:

1. **The deltoid muscles across the scapula.**
2. **The biceps at the front of the humerus.**
3. **The extensor and flexor metacarpi at the front and back of the lower leg.**
4. **The triceps, back of humerus.**
5. **The triceps over the femur.**
6. **The flexor metatarsi at the front of the tibia.**
7. **The gastrocnemius (calf muscle).**
8. **The biceps, back of femur.**
9. **The semitendinosus behind the biceps.**
10. **The gluteus medius from the front to the back of the pelvis.**

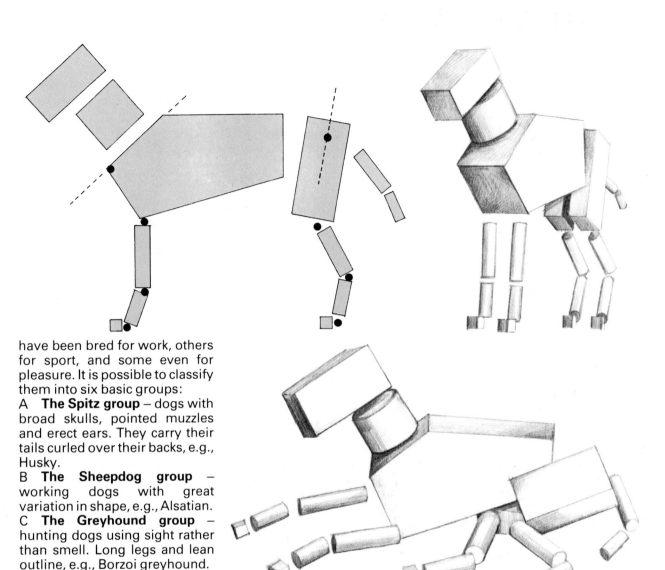

have been bred for work, others for sport, and some even for pleasure. It is possible to classify them into six basic groups:

A **The Spitz group** – dogs with broad skulls, pointed muzzles and erect ears. They carry their tails curled over their backs, e.g., Husky.

B **The Sheepdog group** – working dogs with great variation in shape, e.g., Alsatian.

C **The Greyhound group** – hunting dogs using sight rather than smell. Long legs and lean outline, e.g., Borzoi greyhound.

D **The Hound group** – hunting dogs using smell rather than sight. Long pendant ears, chunky faces, e.g., Basset hound.

E **The Mastiff group** – large bulky dogs, flat muzzles, e.g., Boxer.

F **The Terrier group** – wiry-coated, small to medium size, but strong and hardy, e.g., Airedale.

Above: *The form of a dog simplified into basic geometric volumes. The dotted lines indicate the angle of the shoulder and haunches, while the dots show the main joints.*

Left: *Examples of breeds from each of the six basic groups of dogs.*

Dogs: detail

Obviously, the hair and the details of the soft parts like the nose, ears and eyes, will vary not only from breed to breed but from individual to individual.

The direction of the hair, and the places where it divides or converges, are features worth noting. It is more ordered and complex than is often realized. Look at the front and hind quarters of a short-haired dog like a labrador. In fact, the correct drawing of hair direction can help to indicate form in your drawing. Do not overwork the detail of the hair so the form of the animal is lost. Not every hair needs to be carefully drawn in; suggestion is much better.

Detailed studies of noses, eyes, mouths and paws will be a great help when later drawing from the subject at a distance. They have certain structural characteristics which are common to all dogs, although details and proportions may vary. This is particularly the case with a dog's ears. Basically the ear is a

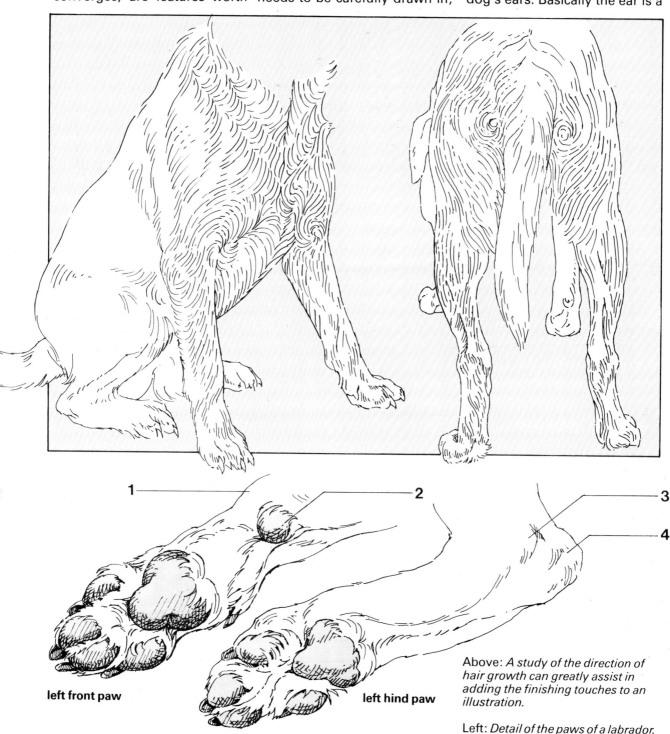

1
2
3
4

left front paw

left hind paw

Above: *A study of the direction of hair growth can greatly assist in adding the finishing touches to an illustration.*

Left: *Detail of the paws of a labrador.*

triangular sheet of cartilage rolled upon itself to form a funnel. In dogs that are always looking about them the ear muscles become highly developed and pricked ears have evolved, but the drooping ear (as in hounds) may be accounted for by underdeveloped muscles.

Key:
1. Carpus
2. Prisiform pad
3. Lower end of fibula
4. Tarsus
5. Fold of ear
6. Eye lid
7. Iris
8. Pupil
9. Nictitating membrane
10. Tear duct
11. Molars
12. Canines
13. Incisors

Below: *Understanding the structure of parts of the body greatly assists when adding detail.*

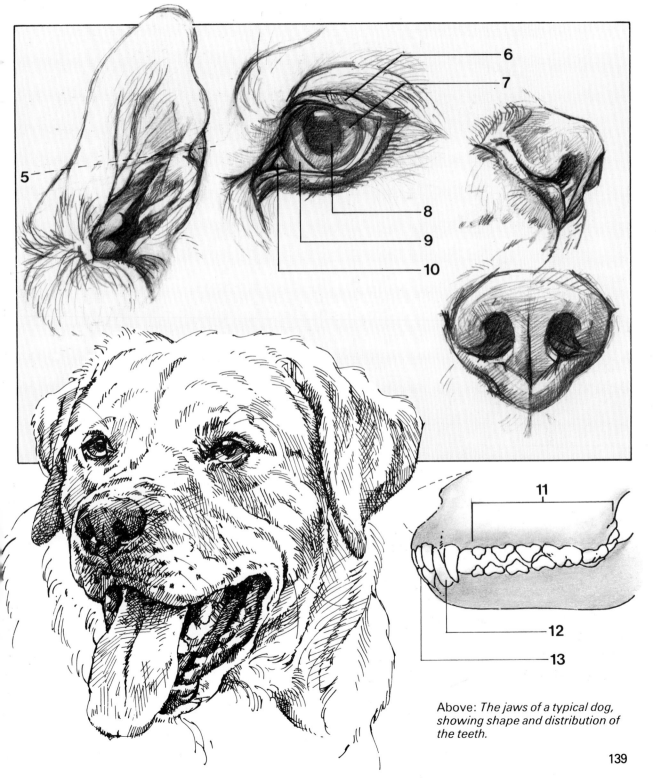

Above: *The jaws of a typical dog, showing shape and distribution of the teeth.*

Dogs: tackling a subject

Above: *An interesting study of a labrador in pen and ink on line board. A scalpel has been used to break up the solidity of the line on the shoulder and paws.*

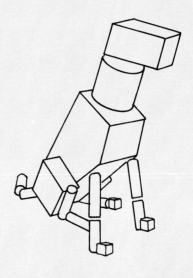

Make sure that both you and your subject are comfortable, you may be willing to suffer for your art, but the dog will not!

The first stage is to create a simplified skeleton on the paper, to correspond with that of the animal.

The volumes are now blocked in. The proportions should be correct at all stages of the procedure.

Left: *Another view, this time in pencil. The alertness of the dog suggests that he is likely to move. You must be ready to accept unfinished drawings.*

These drawings show two different approaches to the same subject: one is drawn in line using ink, and the other is a tonal drawing in pencil.

Drawing directly in ink takes confidence and some practice, as any mark you make is permanent. Mistakes have to be drawn over and incorporated into the drawing, and this makes for a lively result. You can, of course, draw out the construction in pencil, then overdraw in ink, but I think this denies the expressive quality of line unique to a nib. An ink drawing has tremendous strength because of the contrast between the black marks and the white paper. Tone can only be created by building up a texture of lines or dots.

Notice how the direction of the hair has been used to emphasize the form.

In the pencil drawing the form is created by a soft range of greys achieved by delicate shading which follows the direction of the hair or form, whichever appears to be applicable at the time.

The series of drawings below shows the advice given in previous pages put into practice. Mark out a simple bone structure, paying attention to the position of the joints. Using the joints as a guide, draw upon the structure the basic form in simple volumes. Add to and cut away the structure to create a more naturalistic form, taking note of the muscles. Shade in pencil, emphasizing the volume by capturing the play of light across the form. Finally, draw in surface details such as hair direction and individual features such as ears, eyes, nose and feet.

Modify the drawing making the image more life-like by cutting away and adding as necessary.

The basic detail is indicated. If the original drawing is kept light, it will not need erasing.

Tone is added to create a solid and rounded form. This will also help to cover the construction.

Cats: basic structure

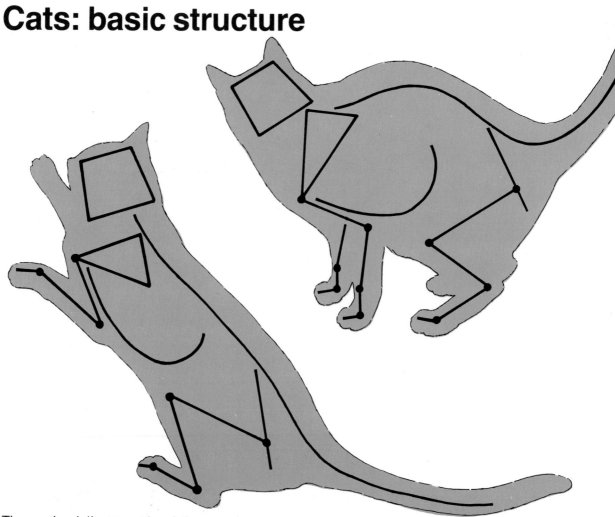

The cat's delicate and subtle proportions demand careful observation and sensitive drawing. The bones are rarely seen at the surface and, in contrast to the angular planes of the dog, a cat typically has a very round and soft, furry form. Very often, the subtle play of light on the fur, or the distortion of its markings, provide the only evidence of the underlying structure.

The cat has a lighter skeleton which is extremely flexible. It can curl up into a tight ball or suddenly appear twice its normal length when making a leap. The cat's legs, particularly its hind ones, are long relative to its body size, and although the cat is therefore extremely fast, it is not designed for prolonged activity. The chest cavity is small and narrow and consequently the heart and lungs are better suited for quick bursts of speed.

Above and opposite above: Drawings of a cat showing how the simplified bone structure works in practice. Note the degree of flexibility of the spine.

Below: Skeleton of a cat showing useful structural landmarks.

Opposite below: The simplified bone structure of a cat. The arrows show the direction of movement at each joint.

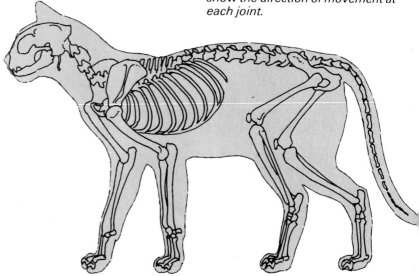

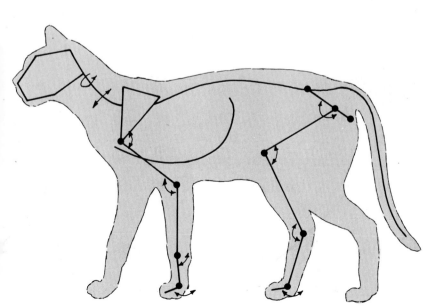

I have drawn a simplified bone structure of the cat. It is very similar to that of the dog. In fact, cats and dogs have the same number of vertebrae. The cat has a slimmer build, being narrower across the shoulders, the pelvis and the chest. The poses above will demonstrate the flexibility of the spine which the dog does not have to the same degree.

The direction and twist of the spine is probably the most important point to establish, followed by the angle of the shoulder blade and the pelvis. The gap between the shoulder blades, which rises above the spine, is particularly noticeable from a back view. The skull is very compact, giving the head a rounded appearance, and the neck is relatively short.

Cats: basic form and movement

Cats are carnivores; their muscles are adapted for freedom of movement. The muscles are especially developed in the back legs – giving a powerful spring – and across the neck and shoulders for striking and carrying prey.

As on pages 140 and 141, these drawings show a simple formula for drawing the form of the animal, and how the rigid volumes can be cut away and shaped to produce a more realistic form.

The sequence of movement shown below is based upon the action photographs of Eadweard Muybridge, and demonstrates how the walk (A-C) is accelerated through the lope (D-F) into a run (J-L).

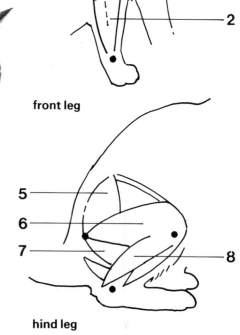

front leg

hind leg

Above: *Detail of the leg muscles.*

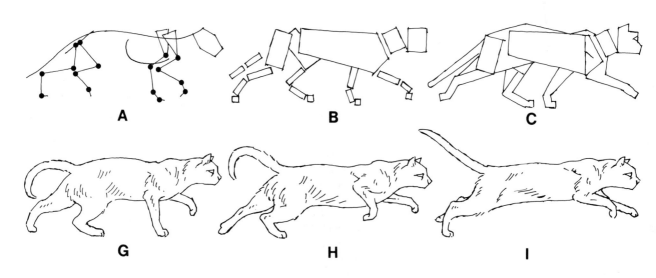

A

B

C

G

H

I

Above: *A. The basic skeleton is drawn in a simplified form.*

B. When the proportions appear correct, build up the volumes of the form.

C. Add further information to clarify the form.

Key:
1. Triceps (front leg)
2. Extensor and flexor metacarpi
3. Biceps (front leg)
4. Deltoid
5. Gluteus medius
6. Triceps (hind leg)
7. Biceps (hind leg)
8. Gastrocnemius

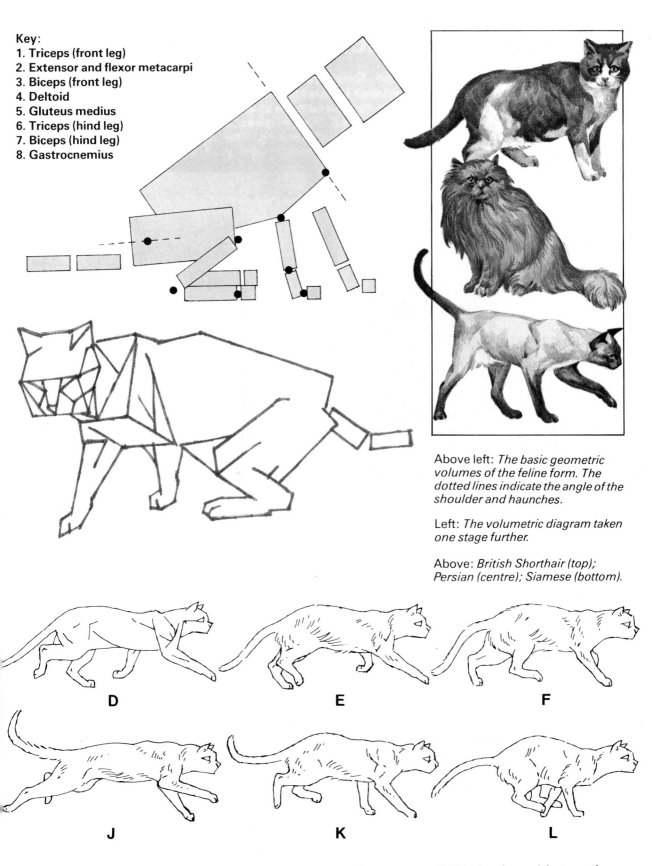

Above left: *The basic geometric volumes of the feline form. The dotted lines indicate the angle of the shoulder and haunches.*

Left: *The volumetric diagram taken one stage further.*

Above: *British Shorthair (top); Persian (centre); Siamese (bottom).*

D

E

F

J

K

L

D. Modify the drawing softening and rounding the shapes to create a more life-like drawing.

E. Finally, indicate the direction of the growth of the fur.

F. This drawing and those on the bottom line (G-L) show the sequence of movement as the walk accelerates to a run.

Cats: detail and tackling a subject

Black and white conté crayon on tinted paper was used for this study of a cat because, when smudged, it will suggest the softness of the fur. Pastel or chalk and charcoal can be used instead. Tonal drawing is good experience for working in paint; in both media you have to work in areas, and this involves a different way of thinking. The tones can be blended with a paper stub or with your finger, but do let the colour and tone of the paper show through in some areas of the drawing. Use the following procedure:

1. With the corner of a white

Above: *Stages in drawing a cat's head, using conté. The method is described in the text.*

Below: *Apply black and white conté to the area required using a "scribbling" motion. The two colours are then blended with a finger.*

conté crayon, draw the basic construction of the head, marking the positions of the ears, eyes, nose and mouth.

2. Lightly shade in the light areas on the face and background, again using white. Using black conté, lay in the details of the markings and features. Also darken the body — particularly under the chin.

3. Work black and white together to produce grey tones, but retain areas of the paper to keep the drawing vital and lively.

No two individual cats of the same breed have identical markings; even the pattern of each side of one individual can vary. There are, however, certain arrangements of blotches, stripes and spots that are shared in certain breeds. The standard tabby pattern has three dark stripes running down the spine, a butterfly pattern across the shoulders and an "oyster" shaped whorl on the flanks. The legs and tail are ringed. The typical face of the tabby is shown opposite. It has a clearly defined pair of "spectacles" around the eyes and on the forehead a mark like the letter "M". The mackerel form of the tabby type has stripes that run around the body, legs and tail, which is probably the reason for the tabby's other name of "tiger cat".

The drawings of the tabby and Siamese heads show the differ- ence in shape between the basic classifications of short-haired cats, the British short-hair and the Foreign short-hair. The other basic group is the long-haired cat or Persian.

The claws of a cat are norm- ally hidden in an opening at the end of the toe so they remain

sharp until needed. There are five claws on each front paw: one claw is placed higher up on the inside of the leg (the dew claw). Four claws are present on the back paws.

left front paw

left hind paw

Left: *One basic difference between the cat varieties is that of proportion. Compare the heads of a British Shorthair (left) with that of a Siamese. You should attempt to get this correct before proceeding further.*

Below left: *Once the proportion is fixed, attention can be paid to the detail, such as the paws. Remember, it is not possible to paint in every hair, so don't even try. Flowing suggestion is far more desirable than exact, but tight, statement.*

right front paw

right hind paw

Horses: basic structure

The modern horse has evolved from a small, lightly built forest-living animal. It had four toes on its front feet and three at the back which splayed out to give it support on the uneven and marshy ground. The third toe was stronger and bore most of the weight. As the animal became larger, the bones between the ankles and the toes lengthened and it began to run on the tip of its toes. It was only when this primitive horse moved onto the firm ground and open grasslands that, through the process of evolution, it began to trot and run on only one toe.

Note, on the illustration top right, that a perpendicular line dropped from the withers passes through the elbow and down the back of the front leg. The shoulder blade is set at approximately 30 degrees to this line. A line produced from the back tendon of each leg extends approximately to the point of the ischium.

A detailed side view of the skeleton is shown in the Introduction to anatomy section. Compare this with the view shown below and see where the bones appear close to the surface.

Key:
1. **The front of the skull (nasal bone).**
2. **The point of the shoulder (top end of humerus).**
3. **The front of the breast bone (sternum).**
4. **The front knee (carpus).**
5. **The rear fetlock (top of phalanges).**
6. **The point of the elbow (extension of the ulna).**
7. **The hind knee (the patella).**
8. **The point of the hock (the extension of the tarsus).**
9. **The hip joint (joint of femur with pelvis).**
10. **The point of the buttock (back end of the pelvis or point of the ischium).**
11. **The point of the croup (front, top end of the pelvis).**
12. **The angle of the haunch (front bottom end of pelvis) or point of ilium.**
13. **The withers (dorsal or thoracic vertebrae).**
14. **Wings of atlas (part of cervical vertebrae).**

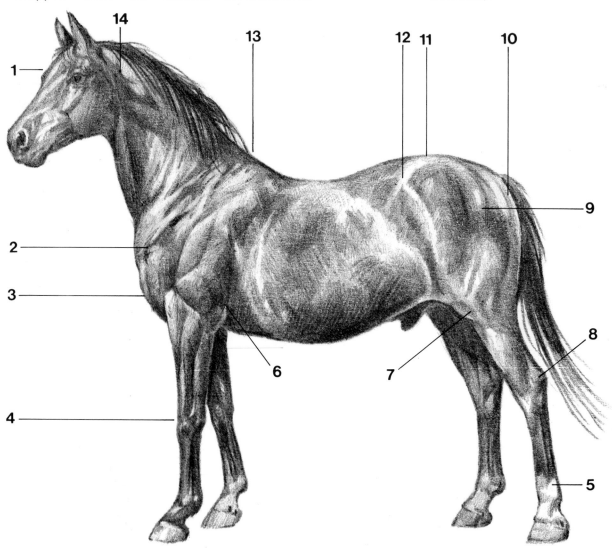

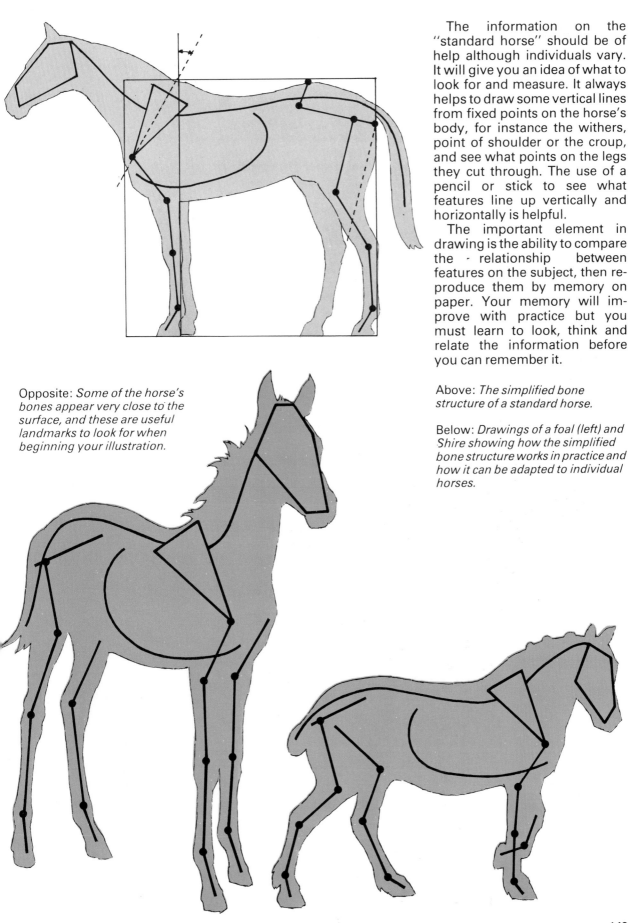

The information on the "standard horse" should be of help although individuals vary. It will give you an idea of what to look for and measure. It always helps to draw some vertical lines from fixed points on the horse's body, for instance the withers, point of shoulder or the croup, and see what points on the legs they cut through. The use of a pencil or stick to see what features line up vertically and horizontally is helpful.

The important element in drawing is the ability to compare the relationship between features on the subject, then reproduce them by memory on paper. Your memory will improve with practice but you must learn to look, think and relate the information before you can remember it.

Above: *The simplified bone structure of a standard horse.*

Below: *Drawings of a foal (left) and Shire showing how the simplified bone structure works in practice and how it can be adapted to individual horses.*

Opposite: *Some of the horse's bones appear very close to the surface, and these are useful landmarks to look for when beginning your illustration.*

Horses: basic form

The muscle structure of a horse is easily observed, the most obvious muscles being indicated on the drawing below. It is even more important to make a careful study of anatomy when drawing horses, as incorrect proportion is immediately noticeable.

The muscles used for running and jumping are well developed. The main masses are concentrated at the buttocks and shoulders and these work the legs by a series of tendons running down and across the leg bones.

The calf muscle (gastrocnemius) is much less obvious than that of the dog as it is overlaid by the massive biceps. Notice also the long vastus, a band of muscle overlying the triceps and biceps. On the forelegs, the triceps are always very obvious.

The diagrams show again how the main body masses can be simplified into box-shaped volumes. The dots mark the main joints. The drawing below this demonstrates how the volumes fit into the more naturalistic body shape.

Key:

1. Supra spinatus
2. Deltoid
3. Biceps
4. Extensor metacarpi
5. Extensor pedis
6. Flexor metacarpi
7. Triceps
8. Flexor metatarsi
9. Flexor perforans
10. Gastrocnemius
11. Biceps
12. Long vastus
13. Semitendinosus
14. Gluteus medius

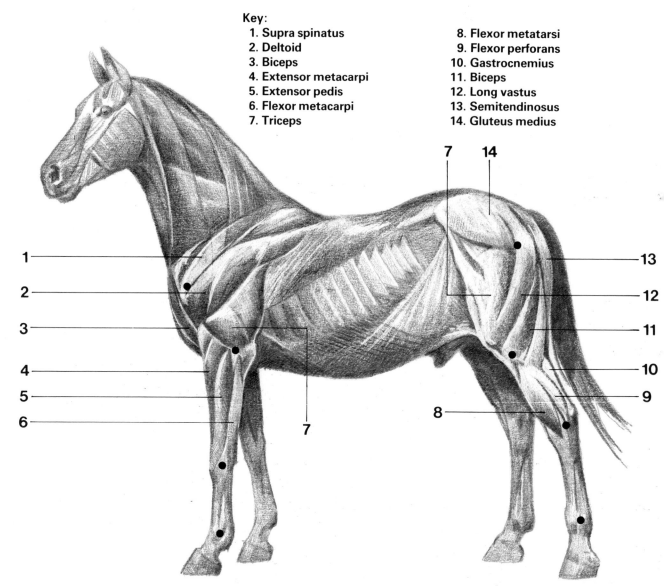

Opposite: *Study of the muscle structure.*

Left: *Stages in drawing a horse's head, progressing from volumetric form to tonal representation.*

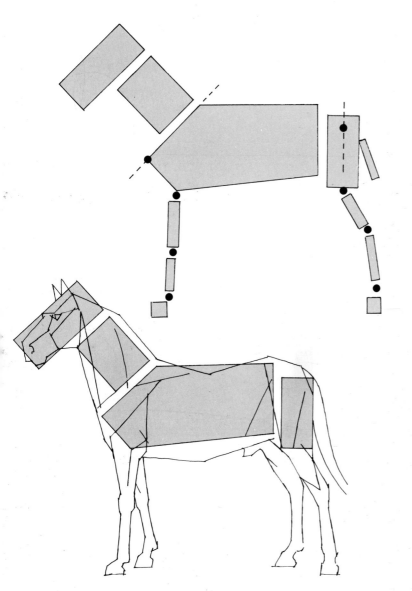

Above centre: *Schematic diagram of a horse showing the joints and important angles.*

Left: *Fitting the volumetric form into a more naturalistic body shape.*

Above: *Drawing of a grazing horse shown in the early stages of its development.*

Horses: tackling a subject

There are many different breeds of horse, varying in size from some of the diminutive ponies, like the Shetland, to massive horses like the Shire. While all breeds share a common skeleton (although the Arab has five lumbar vertebrae instead of the usual six), it is surprising how they can vary so much in shape.

Every horse is differently coloured or marked. Three examples of colour variations are shown, but there are many more. I have also shown some variations in the markings on the face.

The very reflective quality of a shaven dark horse produces

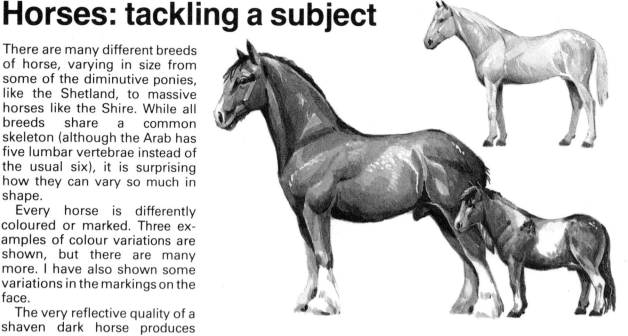

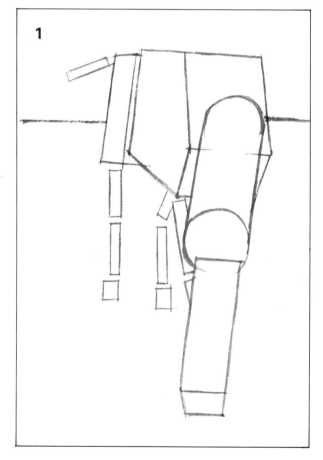

Top and opposite top: *Some of the many different breeds of horse which illustrate individual size and colour variations. Markings on the face are particular to each individual horse and can vary from a white blaze to a white star.*

1

Above: *Mark in the construction of the subject lightly using pencil, charcoal or dilute paint. Adjust the size of the drawing on the paper until you are happy with the composition.*

areas of intense light, particularly on the high spots across the shoulders and haunches and on the flanks where the hair directions conflict. These complications add an interesting challenge to your drawing ability, and mastery of the techniques by which you portray them will increase your drawing skill. To demonstrate the drawing of the horse, black and white paint has been used. It is a good idea to get used to handling paint without the complication of colour mixing and harmonizing. A small chisel brush has been used rather than a pointed one to demonstrate a broad treatment capturing the form of the subject rather than its details.

Above: *Block in the background and general shape of the body with mid grey. Try to use the brush in the direction of the slope of the form. Increase the range of greys working up smaller areas.*

Above: *Paint in the white highlights and darken the shadows. Add some detail but do not go too far, nothing makes a painting less life-like than weighing it down with too much closely observed detail.*

Capturing movement

Walking and running animals are, obviously, very difficult to study without the help of photographs. Even the great animal painters like George Stubbs painted a running horse incorrectly, with all four legs outstretched. The development of photography in the nineteenth century revolutionized the way in which artists portrayed animals in motion.

It was Eadweard Muybridge who, by means of action photography, was able to prove that, during a gallop, a horse draws its feet together, and at one point all four feet leave the ground. His work had a great influence on the cowboy paintings of the American artists Remington and Russell and the horse portraits of Sir Alfred Munnings.

A straight photographic copy, however, is rarely satisfactory as it often captures the move-

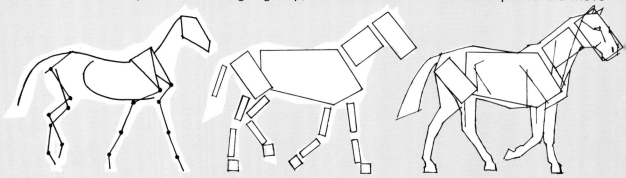

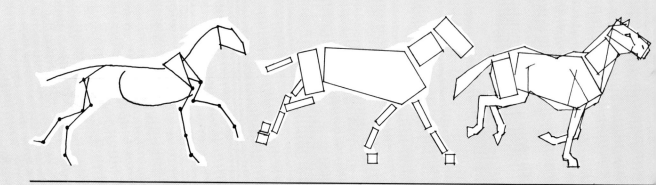

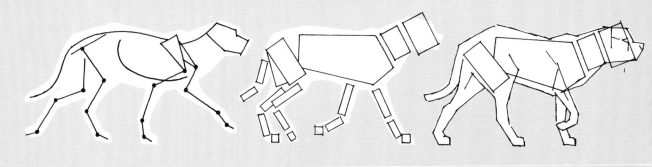

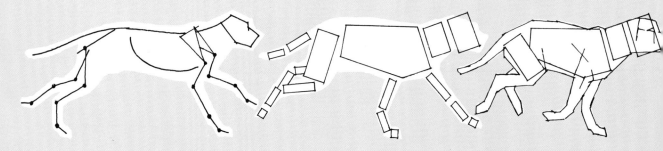

ment at an artistically awkward moment. The feeling of movement of action is best illustrated by portraying the animal in an unbalanced position, for example, with one or more feet off the ground. Try drawing the feet with a little less definition or in a looser manner.

The illustrations below show the drawing methods suggested in this book superimposed on a sequence of photographs by Eadweard Muybridge. The horse and dog are shown walking and running, and the construction shows the progression from the initial axial-skeletal lines through the block form and subsequent stages of refinement to the final use of tone to indicate form.

Below: *Illustrations showing the sequence of movement of a horse and dog in both walking and running attitudes. The basic skeleton is drawn in a simplified form and then information added.*

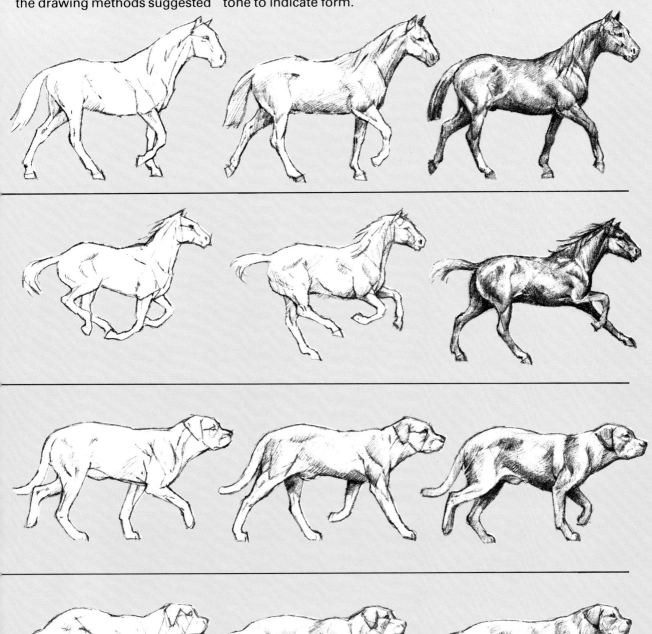

Birds: basic form and structure

More placid birds such as ducks make ideal subjects. You will notice that the skeleton has basic similarities to those of mammals and the bones have the same names.

The shape of a bird is far easier to simplify into geometric shapes – three ovals or ellipses will be enough to suggest the form of most birds. The drawings below illustrate how this is enlarged upon.

In the final drawing, the main feather groups have been indicated. The way the wing feathers overlap when the wing is extended or folded should also be noted. All species have a similar number of wing feathers, although the feathers vary in shape to create the most efficient wing shape for the life style.

Below: *The form of many birds can be suggested by using simple geometric shapes. These are then elaborated upon to give a more defined outline. This can then be worked up using colour. The illustration top left shows the simplified skeleton superimposed over the basic outline.*

Key:
1. **Wing coverts**
2. **Secondaries**
3. **Primaries**
4. **Radius**
5. **Sternum**
6. **Tibia/fibula**
7. **Phalanges**
8. **Metatarsus**
9. **Femur**
10. **Scapula**
11. **Humerus**
12. **Ulna**
13. **Index finger**
14. **Metacarpus**

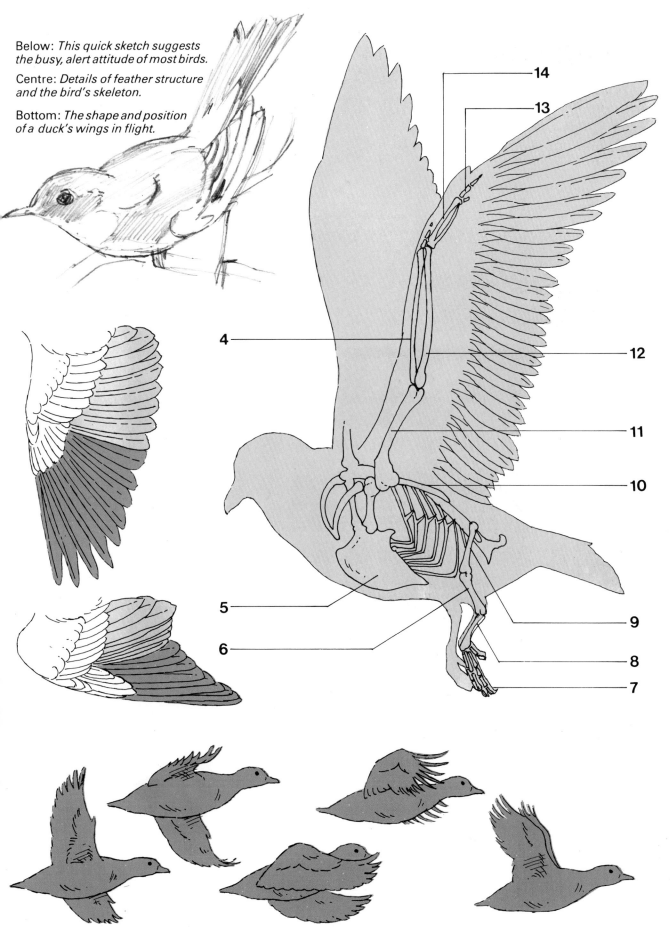

Below: *This quick sketch suggests the busy, alert attitude of most birds.*

Centre: *Details of feather structure and the bird's skeleton.*

Bottom: *The shape and position of a duck's wings in flight.*

14
13
4
12
11
10
5
9
6
8
7

Painting a bird in watercolour

Large birds with a "solid" form like the pelican are much easier to paint from life than small, nervous birds. Both coloured crayon and watercolour – including white – have been used on a light tinted paper.

1. The bird is constructed using the method recommended on page 156. Lines indicate the position of the bill and legs.
2. Using coloured pencil, add to this frame the main shapes of the bill, legs and wings.
3. Some shading is added behind the bird and on its body to suggest is form. More detail is then drawn on the bill and feet.
4. Watercolour is now used to consolidate the solidity and to bring out the shape of the chest and belly.
5. White is used for the first time, to emphasize the form and to make it stand out from the background. The colour of the paper is still allowed to show through on the body.
6. Finally, details of the face, bill and legs are added and the drawing generally made crisper by using a fine brush and sharp crayon or pencil.

This is an ideal combination of media for sketching from life in colour. Do as much drawing as you can with crayon, adding washes of colour if you have time. The late C. F. Tunnicliffe used this technique on tinted paper for his bird sketches.

Painting and drawing birds can be a separate subject in itself. In fact, whatever you find that you prefer to paint will make a suitable point from which to start, because this is exactly what it is – a start. In the end, it is not what you paint that matters, but the work you put into it over the years to increase your experience and expertise.

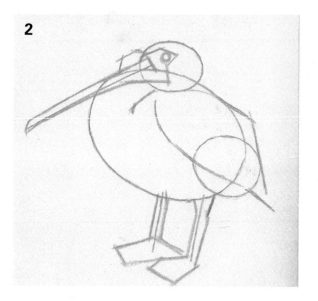

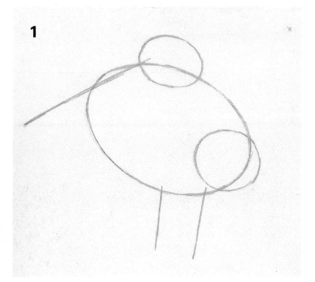

4

5

6

Sketching at the zoo

Because of the generally nervous nature of the animals, much of your drawing from life will remain unfinished, but as you gain confidence you will be able to work with greater speed.

It is a good idea to work on several drawings at the same time, choosing different poses that the subject adopts quite frequently. You will certainly use a lot of paper, but the experience gained in each unfinished sketch will be locked into your memory and will contribute to the standard of your next one. After several drawings, you will be using your growing knowledge of the subject to assist your eyes, and it is difficult to gain this visual experience from photographs.

The drawings on this page are taken from my own sketchbook. Not every drawing works well, for time is so vital that there is no time for erasing or making detailed corrections. I prefer to use a drawing pen with a fine nib and a large capacity of ink. Fine-pointed fountain pens or nylon-tipped pens are also excellent for sketching.